The Ballet Combination Book

By Janet Jerger

Dance Teacher Press
Seward, Nebraska

Library of Congress Control Number: 2009930665
ISBN10: 0-9816586-4-4
ISBN13: 978-0-9816586-4-3
First printing 2004, second printing 2006, third printing 2007, fourth printing 2009

Dance Teacher press

For more information, visit www.DanceTeacherPress.com

Printed in the United States of America

10 9 8 7 6 5 4

The Ballet Combination Book

Contents	Page
Notes	1
Barre	
Plié	3
Tendu	7
Dégagé	13
Rond de Jambe a terre	18
Rond de Jambe en l'air	21
Fondu, Développé	22
Frappé	24
Grand Battement	26
Barre Extras	28
Center	
Port de Bras	29
Adage	30
Center Tendu	33
Body Facings	35
Pas de Bourrée	36
Center Pirouettes	37
Petite Allegro	38
Turns Across the Floor	45
Waltzes	46
Grande Allegro	48
Allegro for Pairs	53
Reverence	54
Floor Turn-Out Exercises	55
Music Suggestions	57
Reproducible Handout	
Simplified Ballet Terms	58

Notes to help you use The Ballet Combination Book

Purpose
This book is designed to give the classroom teacher a multitude of choices and ideas for planning a ballet class. After you have familiarized yourself with The Ballet Combination Book you can easily make class plans or use as a quick reference while teaching. If you need a resources for the definitions of words or the instruction of steps I suggest the following: Ballet Step by Step by Janet Jerger, DanceTeacherPress.com, illustrated definitions of basic ballet terms for students; Technical Manual and Dictionary of Classical Ballet by Gail Grant, not illustrated but very comprehensive; Classical Ballet Technique by Gretchen Ward Warren, an illustrated guide for advanced students.

Music – This book is the perfect companion to the many ballet class CD's available through www.danceclassmusic.com. It is easy to match the categories in this book to the tracks on these CD's. A list of suggested CD's can be found on page 57.

Varied combinations
A good ballet class will be a combination of exercises that are sometimes:
1. Repeated and familiar combinations from past classes so the students get a chance to perfect the movement and see the improvement.
2. New combinations that the student needs to learn quickly. Students need to develop the skill to pick up combinations quickly and remember them immediately.
3. Done at a slow speed to ensure the accuracy and articulation of the feet.
4. Done at a pace that pushes the student to increase quickness.

Balancing
A balance is not written at the end of each exercise, but you should to put a balance on the end of many barre exercises. The beginning student should balance in relevé in 1st, 2nd, 5th, and retiré front. Continue to add relevé balances to your class until you balance in many of these standard positions in every class: sous-sus, retiré front, retiré back, attitude front, attitude back, arabesque, sur le cou de pied, coupé front, and coupé back.

Port de bras
The port de bras that may go with any of these exercises is not always written in the combination unless it is something unique. Using port de bras with the exercise should be added as the student is ready. The beginning student should begin to master the en croix tendu holding the arm in second. Then the standard en croix arm may be added. (5th with the front, 2nd with the side, arabesque with the back, and 2nd with the side) Continue to add varied arm movements as the student progresses.

Port de bras stretches and cambré
To increase the flexibility of your students, include some variation of a port de bras at the end of many or most combinations.
> Port de bras forward and cambré back.
> Circular port de bras.
> Port de bras back and then front. Vary the arms in a port de bras that goes back and then front.
>> A. to start back the arm may go down to low 5th and up to high 5th.
>> B. having the arm in 2nd and reaching straight toward the back to be in cambré back.
> Allongé lunge with port de bras forward and cambré back.
> Stretch side to side.

Class Planning
To plan your class all you have to do is choose your combinations, and make a sticky note!
> Plié #1 – balance in sous-sus
> Tendu #9 - balance in retiré front
> Dégagé #3
> Rond de Jambe #2 – balance in arabesque
> Frappé #5 – balance in coupé front
> Battement #7 Etc.

Body facings – body positions from the Cecchetti school, see page 35.

Positions of the feet – are the same in all schools so the terminology should not be a problem.

Positions of the arms – Arms positions noted are French which are commonly used.

1st - in front of the chest – en avant
2nd - to the side
3rd - one in 2nd and the other in 5th (unless middle 3rd where the 5th arm is in 1st)
4th - one arm in 1st and one in 5th
5th - both arms high - en haut

Arabesque arms – arms in 1st and 2nd arabesque are the same in all schools.

I also like to use the Cecchetti 3rd arabesque arms where both arms are forward from the shoulder, the downstage arm is horizontal and the upstage arm is up 45°. This arm is suggested with many steps such as temp lié, grand jeté, and sissonne.

Abbreviations and terms

Upstage, downstage, stage right, and stage left = US, DS, SR, SL
Front and Back: f=front, b=back.
Right and Left: R=right, L=left
Other side means right becomes left.
Reverse means front becomes back.

Failli: the failli referred to in this book is simply when the leg extended to the back in arabesque comes through first to fourth in front.
Glissade: Unless specified glissade will be *glissade derrière* which moves to the side commencing with the back foot and closing front.
Jeté: Unless specified jeté will be *jeté dessus* (jeté over). The back foot will brush in a frappé à la seconde, spring off the floor, land on that foot with the other foot in cou de pied back.
Pas de Chat: Unless specified the pas de chat should commence with the back foot and close front.
Pas de Bourrée: Unless specified the pas de bourrée will be under: back, side, front.

Corners: C1, C2, C3, and C4 indicate the directions corner 1, corner 2, etc.

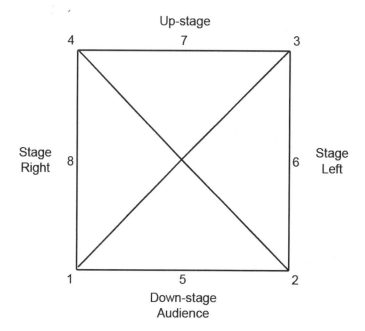

Plié

1. 16 counts in 4 positions, pliés and port de bras

1st	1-2	demi plié (arm from 2nd to low)
	3-4	demi plié (arm en avant and open 2nd)
	5-8	grand plié
	1-8	port de bras forward and port de bras back
2nd	1-4	2 demi plié
	5-8	grand plié
	1-8	port de bras to the barre, then away from the barre
4th	1-4	2 demi plié
	5-8	grand plié
	1-4	tendu front, plié, port de bras forward
	5-8	stay tendu front, straight supporting leg, port de bras back
5th	1-4	2 demi plié
	5-8	grand plié
	1-8	grand port de bras -en dehors and en dedans

* to add an additional 16 counts in each position

1-8   relevé 1, lower 2, relevé 3, lower 4, relevé 5, lower 6, relevé 7 and hold (arm low, 1st, 5th, 2nd)

1-8   hold the balance 1-6, lower 7, change to next position 8

2. 16 count in 4 positions, pliés and port de bras (begin in 2nd, then 1st, 4th, 5th)

1-4	2 demi plié (arm to 1st and open 2nd with each)
	* variation (arm to 1st open 2nd, arm to 5th open 2nd)
5-8,1-4	2 grand plié
5-8	2nd - port de bras to the barre, down to the front and up
	1st - port de bras forward
	4th – grand port de bras en dehors
	5th - grand port de bras en dedans

ending- demi plié in fifth position, relevé with retiré front, balance 8 counts

3. 16 counts in 4 positions, 2 grand with port de bras

2nd position	1-4	grand plié, with first port de bras,
	5-8	grand plié, with inward port de bras
	1-4	port de bras side to the barre, down through the front and recover
	5-8	port de bras side to the barre, going to the back and recover
1st position	1-8	2 grand plié, 1 with standard 1st port de bras,
		2nd with inward port de bras
	1-8	port de bras forward and to the back
4th position	1-8	2 grand plié, 1 with standard 1st port de bras,
		2nd with inward port de bras
	1-4	port de bras side to the barre, and recover
	5-8	port de bras side away from the barre and recover
5th position	1-8	2 grand plié, 1 with standard 1st port de bras,
		2nd with inward port de bras
	1-8	port de bras forward and to the back

4. 2 grand, port de bras, relevé

2nd position	1-8	2 grand plié
	1-4	port de bras forward
	5-8	relevé balance
1st position	1-8	2 grand plié
	1-4	port de bras forward
	5-8	relevé balance
4th position	1-8	2 grand plié
	1-4	tendu front, plié, port de bras forward
	5-8	straight knees, port de bras back
5th position	1-8	2 grand plié
	1-4	port de bras side, to the barre, down through front to recover
	5-8	port de bras side, to the barre, through the back to recover

piqué forward to sous-sus, arms high 5th balance for 8 or 16, finish

3

Plié

5. <u>Demi, relevé, demi, relevé, grand, port de bras</u>

16 counts in each position

1-2	demi plié
3-4	relevé and lower
5-6	demi plié
7-8	relevé and lower
1-4	grand plié
5-8	port de bras forward in 1st
	port de bras to the barre in 2nd
	port de bras away from the barre in 4th
	port de bras to the back

ending
	1-2	demi
	3-4	sous-sus
	5-8	front leg up to passé
	1-8	balance and finish

6. <u>Plies 32 counts in each position – arm low</u>

1-4	2 demi, arm breathes
5-8	grand plié with inward port de bras
1-4	port de bras forward, leave arm high
5-8	relevé balance, arms in high 5th, finish arm low
1-16	repeat with port de bras back

7. <u>Plié begin parallel - 24 counts x 4 positions + 16 ct ending</u>

1-4	2 demi plié
5	demi plié down
6-7	turn-out in plié
8	straighten
1-8	2 grand plié
1-8	port de bras: front and back in 1st
	to the barre, away from the barre in 2nd
	away from the barre, to the barre in 4th
	front and back in 5th

ending:
	1-8	sous-sus in 5th, port de bras front and back
	1-8	balance on relevé in retiré front

8. <u>Plié with wrap balance 32 ct x 4 positions</u>

begin in 1st

1-4	grand plié
5-8	relevé balance
1-4	grand plié
5-8	2 demi plié

1-8	port de bras:	1st	front and back
		2nd	to the barre, away from the barre
		4th	tendu front with plié port de bras forward, straighten supporting leg, port de bras back
		5th	front and back

1-2	relevé
3-4	turn torso toward the barre wrapping arms around waist
5-6	open arms back to seconde
7-8	lower and change position

repeat in 2nd, 4th , and 5th position

9. 24 counts in 3 positions, pliés with special port de bras

1st position	1-2	demi plié, arm down and to 1st
	3-4	demi plié, arm open 2nd and raise 45° from shoulder (allongé)
	5-8	arm only port de bras, down, 1st, high 5th, open 2nd
	1-8	2 grand plié
	1-8	port de bras forward and backward
2nd position	1-16	same as in 1st
	1-4	slow port de bras side to the barre
	5-8	then forward with plié, recover arm to seconde
5th position	1-16	same as in 1st
	1-2	port de bras forward, stay down
	3-4	palms down, demi-plié, straighten legs staying forward
	5-6	again demi-plié, straighten
	7-8	roll up to a standing position

10. Plié - 24 counts in 4 positions plus ending balance

1-4	demi (arm low 5th, 1st), demi (arm high 5th, open seconde)
5-8	grand plié (1st port de bras)
1-4	grand plié (regular port de bras again, or inside port de bras)
5-8	relevé, plié, relevé, plié

1-8	port de bras	1st	port de bras forward and back
		2nd	port de bras to the barre and away
		4th	tendu front plié (fondu),
			port de bras forward, straight knee to the back
		5th	grand port de bras en dehors, en dedans
1-16	ending		sous-sus balance

11. Plié with little demi stretches

The first three counts are 3 little demi plié that do not straighten in between.

1	demi lift outside heel to the ball of the foot
2	demi plié and point the toe leaving it in same placement
3	demi back to the ball of the foot
4	straighten in 1st, stretching behind the knees
5-8	same as 1-4 with inside leg
1-4	grand plié
5-8	grand plié
1-4	port de bras forward
5-8	relevé

repeat in 2nd, 4th and 5th

12. Pliés and relevés with stretches after 4 positions

1	demi plié - arm to low 5th
2	relevé – arm to high 5th
3-4	other arm up and balance
5-6	demi, relevé leaving the arms high
7-8	lower to flat, arms to seconde
1-4	grand plié
5-8	change to next position

after all the positions go back to 1st

1-16	port de bras forward 4, hang for 8, roll up for 4
1-8	port de bras forward and to the back
1-8	port de bras to the barre and away
1-8	demi plié, relevé to retiré and balance

Plié

13. Pliés with longer balances
1-2	demi plié - arm to 1st and open 2nd
3-6	grand plié
7-8	demi plié – arm to 5th and open 2nd
1-2	press up to relevé – arm low to 5th
3-4	barre arm matches – low to 5th
5-8,1-2	balance
3-4	lower heels and open arms
5-8	tendu to the next position
1-24	same in 2nd
1-24	same in 4th
1-24	same in 5th, end tendu takes you back to 1st
1-16	grand port de bras en dehors then en dedans
1-16	sous-sus and repeat port de bras
1-16	pick front leg up to coupé front and balance

14. Plié with extra stretch
1-4	grand plié with 1st port de bras
5-8	grand plié with inside port de bras
1-2	port de bras forward, stay there
3-4	both hands down touching floor
5-6	demi plié while forward
7-8	straighten legs
1-2	demi plié again
3-4	straighten legs
5-6	demi plié
7-8	straighten legs and roll up straightening torso

repeat in 2nd and 5th

15. Plié with forced arch
1	demi plié down
2	lift your heels in plié forcing a good arch
3	straighten up to relevé
4	lower the heels
5-8	grand plié
1-4	port de bras front
5-8	press up relevé, come down change to 2nd on 8
1-8	repeat the first 1-8 in 2nd
1-4	port de bras to the barre
5-8	press up relevé, come down change to 4th on 8
1-8	repeat the first 1-8 in 4th
1-4	port de bras away from the barre
5-8	press up relevé, come down change to 5th on 8
1-8	repeat the first 1-8 in 5th
1-4	port de bras to the back
5-8	sous-sus and lift leg to attitude front
1-8	balance in attitude, stretch leg devant, wrists lengthening before closing

16. End balance that switches sides and teaches en dehors turn
* use at the end of any combination
1-2	with R foot front in 5th demi plié
3-4	relevé passé with a half - turn to the L, L will be in retiré front
5-8	balance with arms in 1st or 5th
1-8	balance longer and finish ready for the other side

> **Note:** Most tendu CD bands are 64 counts long.
> I have given 3 basic tendu exercises that are each 32 counts long for beginners.
> For intermediate students use one of the 32 ct combinations plus basic A or basic B.
> (This combines a more complex combination with a basic concentrating on technique.)
> For more advanced dancers use 2 of the intermediate 32 counts linked together.
> Many of the combinations could be done once from 1st position and repeat in 5th position.

Basic Tendu A - 4 tendu en croix
1-8	4 tendu front
1-8	4 tendu side (closing f,b,f,b)
1-8	4 tendu back
1-8	4 tendu side (closing b,f,b,f)

* variation - close each tendu in plié

Basic Tendu B - 1 tendu en croix 4 times
1-8	1 front, 1 side, 1 back, 1 side
1-24	repeat 3 times

* variation - close each tendu in plié

Basic Tendu C - 32 counts
1-8	4 tendu front
1-8	4 tendu back-inside leg
1-8	4 tendu side changing
1-8	4 tendu side closing with plié (changing)

1. Tendu with fondu – 32 counts - en croix
1	plié
2	tendu, staying in plié
3	close, staying in plié
4	straighten
5-16	continue en croix
1-2	fondu front, close (tendu with plié, close straight)
3-4	fondu side, close
5-6	fondu back, close
7-8	fondu side, close
1-8	repeat last 8

2. Tendu with heel down – 32 counts
1	tendu front
2	heel down
3	point
4	close
5	tendu side
6	close front plié
7	tendu side
8	close back straight
1-8	reverse
1-16	repeat all

3. Tendu 32 counts
1-4	4 tendu front
5-8	4 tendu back
1-4	2 tendu front, 2 tendu back
5-8	3 tendu side close 1st, 1 tendu side close back
Reverse	

Tendu

4. Tendu with relevé- 32 counts
1	tendu front, arm in seconde
2	plié in 4th, arm in first
3	relevé in 4th
4	plié in 4th
5	relevé in 4th
6	plié in 4th
7	stretch to tendu front, arm opens to 2nd
8	close 5th
1-8	repeat to the side with plié in 2nd, arm stays in seconde
1-8	repeat to the back with plié in 4th, arm same as with the front
1-8	repeat to the side with plié in 2nd

5. Tendu with flex - en croix – 32 counts
1-4	tendu, turn-in, turn-out, flex w/plié
5-8	tendu, plié in 4th (or 2nd), tendu, close

6. Tendu with flex and turn-in - en croix – 32 counts
1	tendu
2	flex
3	point
4	turn in
5	turn out
6	close
7-8	tendu, close plié

7. Tendu with heel down for turn-out – en croix - 32 counts
1-4	tendu, heel down, tendu, close
5-6	tendu, heel down
7-8	pull into 5th keeping whole foot on the ground

8. Tendu with flex and heel down – 48 counts
front	1-4	tendu, heel down, tendu, close
	5-8	tendu, flex, tendu, close
back	1-8	same
side	1-8	tendu, heel down, tendu, flex, tendu, heel down, tendu close back
	1-24	reverse

9. Tendu in an open and closed position in 1st – 32 counts
front	1	tendu front- open *
	2	slide tendu to a crossed position, (thighs touch)
	3	slide tendu back to open position
	4	close 1st
	+5	tendu front, close
	+6	tendu front, close
	+7,8	tendu front, close plié
side	1-4	tendu side, plié in 2nd, tendu, close 1st
	+5,+6, +7-8	3 tendu side, last one close plié
back	1-8	like front
side	1-8	repeat side

* If you point your tendu straight in front of where your heel was in 1st position, your tendu is open. If you point in front of the arch of the supporting foot, you are in a closed position which is more beautiful and gives you more stretch.

10. Tendu with turn-in, flex, and ball of foot – 32 counts

front	1-4	tendu, turn-in, turn-out, flex and plié
	5	straighten supporting leg, stretch foot point tendu
	6	pull toes back so ball of the foot is on the ground
	7	point tendu
	8	close
side	1-4	tendu side, plié in 2nd, tendu, close-b
	5-8	4 tendu side close f,b,f,b
back	1-8	like front
side	1-4	tendu side, plié in 2nd, tendu, close f
	5-8	4 tendu side closing b,f,b,f

11. Tendu with inside leg – 32 counts

1,2	tendu front, close
3,4	tendu front, close
+5,+6	2 quick tendu front
+7	inside leg tendu back close
+8	inside leg tendu side, close front
1-8	reverse
1-4	tendu side close back, tendu side close front
+5,+6+7+8	3 tendu side closing 1st, 1 tendu side close back
1-4	tendu side close front, tendu side close back
+5+6+7+8	3 tendu side close 1st, 1 tendu side close front

12. Tendu with temp lié – 32 counts

1	tendu front
2	temp lié forward (through 4th plié)
3	tendu back
4	temp lié back
5	tendu front
6	close
+7	tendu front, close
+8	tendu front, close
24	continue en croix, side temps lie through 2nd away from barre then back to the barre

13. Tendu with coupé – 32 counts

1-3	3 tendu front
4	petite passé with inside leg (pick up to coupé and change)
5-7	3 tendu back
8	petit passé with inside leg
1-3	3 tendu side changing
4	petit passé with inside leg
5-7	3 tendu side changing
8	inside leg coupé without changing
1-16	reverse

14. Tendu with pas de cheval - en croix – 64 counts

1-4	4 tendu
5-8	4 pas de cheval out
1-4	4 tendu
5-8	4 pas de cheval in (enveloppé)

15. Tendu with passé – 16 counts

+1,+2	2 tendu front, accent in
+3	tendu front, close plié
+4	passé close back
5-8	reverse
1-8	tendu close plié, en croix, with port de bras

Tendu

16. Tendu with pas de cheval –32 counts each side

1	slide foot from 5th position to 1st position
2	slide to back 5th plié
3	slide to 1st
4	slide to front 5th plié
5-6	pas de cheval front straightening supporting leg, close 5th
7-8	tendu front, close 5th
1-8	repeat first 8 with pas de cheval side close front, tendu side close back
1-8	repeat with pas de cheval and tendu to the back
1	tendu back
2	cloche to tendu front
3	plié in fourth
4	push turning toward the barre into tendu front on the other side
5-6	step forward sous-sus
7-8	lower

continue other side

17. Tendu with passé – 32 counts or 64 with repeat

1,2	tendu front, close
3,4	passé change, passé change
5,6	tendu side, close back
7,8	passé change, passé change
1,2	tendu back, close
3,4	passé change, passé change
+5	tendu back
+6	tendu side change
+7	tendu front
+8	tendu side change
1-16	reverse
1-32	repeat entire exercise

18. Tendu with coupé 16 counts, 32 with repeat

1	tendu front ouverte
2	close 5th
+3	tendu side, close 1st
+4	tendu side, close 5th back
+5,+6.+7	3 tendu back, al of them closing into coupé back
+8	tendu back, close 5th
1-8	reverse
1-16	repeat all

19. Tendu with coupé fondu and balance

to the front

1-4	2 tendu
5	fondu with coupé
6	stretch out to tendu
7-8	fondu with coupé, close 5th

to the back

1-8	same with the inside leg to the back

to the side

1-4	2 tendu side
5	fondu with coupé front
6	stretch to tendu side
7	fondu in coupé back
8	rise to relevé in coupé back and
1-8	hold balance

reverse

20. <u>Tendu with ball of the foot</u> This combination works on the tendu technique. For example the tendu front should begin by leading with the heel and begin closing tendu by pulling the toes back. To place the ball of the foot down in front the toes should be pulled back, not the body rocked forward to put weight on the foot.

1-32	1-8 en croix	1	tendu
		2	ball of the foot (pull toes back)
		3	stretch to tendu
		4	ball of the foot
		5	stretch to tendu
		6	ball of the foot
		7	stretch to tendu
		8	close
1-16	part b		2 tendu en croix with port de bras
1-16	part c	1-3	3 side tendu to first
		4	side close 5th back
		5-7	3 side tendu to first
		8	side close 5th front
		1-8	repeat last 8 counts

21. <u>Rond de jambe- tendu combo</u>

1	tendu front
2	plié in 4th
3	straighten back to tendu front
4	ronde de jambe to the back
5	through first to the front
6	close front
7	tendu side
8	close back
1-8	reverse
1-8	tendu with plié en croix
1-8	repeat

22. <u>Tendu with unique pattern</u>

1	tendu front
2	close 5th
3	tendu front
4	close 5th
5	tendu front
6	plié in 4th
7	relevé in 4th
8	plié in 4th
1	tendu front
2	close
3	tendu front
4	close
5	tendu front
6	close
7	demi plié
8	straighten knees
1-16	same to the side
1-16	to the back
1-16	to the side

Tendu

23. <u>Tendu with heel down</u>

1	tendu à la seconde
2	lower heel in seconde
3	raise heel again to be in tendu
4	lower heel in seconde
5	pointe inside leg to tendu
6	lower inside heel
7	pointe inside toe again
8	lower heel in seconde
1	pointe outside foot
2	close 5th front
3-4	tendu front and close
5-6	tendu side, close back
7-8	tendu back and close

Now repeat, the first 8 will stay the same, the second half will close back and then tendu b,s,f.

---

* * Teaching Tip - Getting the most out of your time. * *
One way to save time and give your students all their required elements
is to use the same combination for tendu and dégagé and perhaps grand battement.
Less time demonstrating and more time working.

---

24. <u>Tendu – that can be repeated as dégagé</u>

1-4	2 tendu devant
5-8	2 tendu derrière (inside leg)
1-4	2 tendu à la seconde both closing devant
5-8	2 tendu à la seconde both closing derrière
1-4	2 tendu derrière
5-8	2 tendu devant (inside leg)
1-4	2 tendu à la seconde both closing derrière
5-8	2 tendu à la seconde both closing devant
1-8	4 tendu à la seconde closing first (arm goes en dehors)
1-8	4 tendu à la seconde closing first (arm goes en dedans)
1-8	port de bras forward
1-8	cambré back
1-12	sous-sus and balance
1-4	détourné and lower for other side

25. <u>Tendu with demi-ronde</u>

1	tendu front
2	close 5th
3	tendu front
4	demi ronde to the side
5	close 5th front
6	tendu side
7-8	close back and hold
1	tendu back
2	close 5th
3	tendu back
4	demi ronde to à la seconde
5	close 5th back
6	tendu side
7-8	close front and hold

12

Dégagé in 1st

1. The Classic - face the barre - all dégagés to the side
>
> 1-16   8 right, 8 left
>
> 1-8   4 right, 4 left
>
> 1-8   2 right, 2 left, 1 right, 1 left, 1 right, 1 left

* one set holding the barre, repeat with arms in 2nd
* also use this combination in the center, one set arms in 2nd, repeat with arms 5th

1a. The Classic continued - face the barre - all dégagés to the side
* one set of the classic above and seconde set closing 5th described below
>
> 1-8   8 right, closing bfbfbfbf
>
> 1-8   8 left, closing fbfbfbfb
>
> 1-8   4 right, 4 left continue pattern with every dégagé changing
>
> 1-4   2 right, 2 left
>
> 5-8   1 right, 1 left, 1 right, 1 left - all closing back

2. Face the barre
>
> 1-8   8 dégagé right to the side
>
> 1   tendu side
>
> 2   plié in seconde
>
> 3   relevé
>
> 4   plié
>
> 5   relevé
>
> 6   plié
>
> 7   tendu
>
> 8   close 1st
>
> now left, repeat all

3. Dégagé and piqué face the barre
>
> 1-8   8 dégagé side with the right
>
> 1-8   8 dégagé side with the left
>
> 1-4   4 piqué right (leg stiffly out à la seconde tapping floor with toe)
>
> 5-7   stretch leg out in dégagé
>
> 8   close
>
> 1-8   repeat last 8 to the left
>
> 1-8   4 sets of plié, relevé
>
> 1-8   stay in relevé balance, lower on 8

4. Dégagé and en cloche (dégagé out on + and close on the count)
>
> 1-3   3 dégagé side in first
>
> +4   relevé in first, lower
>
>   en cloche
>
> +   front
>
> 1   back
>
> 2   front
>
> 3   back
>
> 4   first
>
> 1   dégagé side, close 5th front
>
> 2   dégagé side, close 1st
>
> 3   dégagé side, close 5th back
>
> 4   dégagé side, close 1st
>
> 5-8   repeat last 1-4
>
> 1   tendu side
>
> 1-2   prepare in 4th position back with plié
>
> 3-4   en dehors pirouette
>
> 5-8   stop by putting hand on barre, and balancing in retiré devant on relevé
>
> 1-6   continue balancing, 7-8 lower to first position
>
> repeat all

Dégagé in 1st

5. **A basic**
1-4	ball of the foot (lifting heel), point (lifting knee) toe stays, ball, plié
5-8	4 dégagé side
1-8	repeat with inside leg
1-8	2 dégagé f, 2s, 2b, 2s
1-8	8 dégagé side with an outward port de bras
1-8	8 dégagé side with an inward port de bras
1-16	16 en cloche

6. **Dégagé and retiré en croix** (put weight on both feet in first)
1-4	dégagé front, close 1st, retiré, close 1st
5-8	same to the side
1-4	same to the back
5-8	same to the side
1	dégagé ouverte to the side
2	plié in seconde arms down
3	relevé arms to 5th
4-8,1-4	balance in relevé
5	plié in seconde
6	back to dégagé side position
7-8	close 1st

7. **Piqué and en cloche** (these piqués are a stretched leg tapping the floor sharply)
1-24	8 piqué front, 8 piqué side, 8 piqué back
1-8	7 piqué side, close 1st
1-16	16 en cloche beginning front
1-16	15 en cloche with arms high 5th, close 1st

Dégagé in 5th

8. **Basic**
1-16	4 dégagé en croix
1-8	8 dégagé à la seconde in first with en dehors arm
1-8	8 dégagé à la seconde in first with en dedans arm

9. **Dégagé à la seconde**
A	1-8	7 side closing 1st, 8th to the side close back
	1-8	7 side closing 1st, 8th to the side close front
B	1-2	2 side closing 1st
	+3	2 quick to the 1st
	4	1 to the side close back
	5-8	1st, 1st, quick, quick, front
B	1-8	repeat B

10. **Dégagé with piqué**
1-4	tendu front, carry side (demi-ronde), carry front, close
5-8	2 dégagé front, dégagé side close front, dégagé side close back
1-8	reverse
1-4	piqué, front, side, front, close
5-8	2 dégagé front, dégagé side close front, dégagé side close back
1-8	reverse

11. Dégagé with en cloche

1-4	4 dégagé front
5-7	en cloche front, back, front
8	close
1-8	4 tendu side with plié closing, f, b, f, b
1-16	reverse

12. Dégagé with en cloche - 32 counts

+1	dégagé front, close
+2	dégagé front, close
+3	dégagé front, brush back
+4	brush front, close front
+5	dégagé side, close back
+6	dégagé side, close front
+7	2 dégagé to first
+8	dégagé side, close back
continue back and side, repeat all	

13. Dégagé with piqué - 32 counts

1-4	piqué f, s, b, brush through to front
5	close
+6	dégagé side, close back
+7, 8	dégagé back, close plié
1-8	reverse
1-16	4 dégagé en croix

14. Dégagé with turn-in

1-4	coupé, turn-in across other leg, back to coupé, extend 2nd
5-8	4 dégagé side
1-8	repeat
1-8	dégagé f, s, b, plié
1-8	dégagé b, s, f, plié
1-8	8 dégagé side with an outward port de bras
1-8	8 dégagé side with an inward port de bras

15. Dégagé with a fun pattern

A	1-3	R - dégagé f, s, b
	4	L - inside leg dégagé f
	5-7	R – dégagé b, s, f
	8	L - inside leg b
B	1	R - dégagé f
	2	L - passé back to front
	3	L - passé front to back
	4	R – dégagé f
	5	L - dégagé b
	6	R – passé front to back
	7	R - passé back to front
	8	L – dégagé b
C	1	R – dégagé f
	2	L – dégagé b
	3	R – dégagé side close 1st
	4	R – dégagé side close back
	5	R – dégagé back
	6	L – dégagé front
	7	R – dégagé side close 1st
	8	R – dégagé side close front
C	1-8	repeat C

Dégagé in 5th

16. Dégagé with glissade for allegro work

1-4	4 dégagé front closing in plié
5	glissade forward
6	dégagé front
7	glissade back
8	dégagé back (inside leg)
1	glissade change away from barre
2	dégagé side from back to front
3	glissade change to the barre
4	dégagé inside leg side from front to back
5-8	repeat last 1-4
1-16	repeat from the beginning
1-8	passé balance
1-2	draw passé down leg to stand in sous-sus
3-4	détourné
5-8	demi plié, straighten finish

17. Dégagé with fondu and en cloche

1-4	4 dégagé front
5	dégagé front out
6	coupé plié (fondu)
7	développé front
8	close
1-8	repeat to the side
1-8	repeat to the back
1-2	dégagé back
3-4	cloche front
5	cloche back
6	cloche front
7	cloche back
8	close back
1-32	reverse all

18. Fast dégagé

A	1-3	piqué touch f, s, b
	4	close back
	5-7	piqué b, s, f
	8	close front
A	1-8	repeat A
B		dégagés to the side
	1	close back
	2	close front
	3-4	close back plié
	5	close front
	6	close back
	7-8	close front plié
B	1-8	repeat B
C	1-8	8 degage side closing 1st with an outside port de bras
C	1-8	8 degage side closing 1st with an inside port de bras
D	1-8	demi, relevé 4 times, stay in relevé
	1-8	balance on relevé in 1st for 7 counts, lower finish on 8

19. <u>**Dégagé and passé**</u> (all the passés are done with the inside leg)

1-3	3 dégagé devant
4	passé (inside leg back to front)
5-7	3 dégagé side changing
8	passé (inside leg back to front)
1-3	3 dégagé derrière
4	passé (inside leg front to back)
5-7	3 dégagé side changing
8	passé (inside leg front to back)
1-3	push up to relevé retiré front and hold
4	plié in 5th
5-7	relevé again up to retiré front (pirouette position)
8	plié in 5th
1-3	en dehors pirouette
4	plié in 5th
5-8	en dehors pirouette and stay in relevé retiré
1-16	move leg to attitude back and balance

20. <u>**Pas de cheval and dégagé**</u>

1-4	2 pas de cheval devant
5	dégagé front ouverte
6	pull into coupé (sur le cou de pied)
7	extend back out to dégagé
8	close
1-8	same to the side
1-8	same to the back
1	tendu back
2	through first to tendu front
3	plié in fourth
4	pivot toward the barre into tendu front
5-6	piqué forward into sous-sus
7-8	lower and ready for other side

21. <u>**Dégagé accent in and frappé accent out**</u>

1-3	3 dégagé devant and close 5th
4	1 dégagé devant close sur le cou de pied
5-7	3 frappé devant
8	close 5th
1-8	repeat to the side
1-8	repeat derrière
1-2	tendu side
3-4	preparation 4th derrière plié
5-6	en dehors pirouette
7-8	closes back
1-32	reverse the combination, the last 8 counts stay the same with an en dehors don't close
1-4	balance in retiré front where your pirouette ended
1-12	change to attitude front and balance

Rond de Jambe a terre

1. Rond de jambe

1-8	3 ½ slow en dehors rond de jambe (f on 1,b,f,b,f,b,f hold)
1-8	3 slow en dedans (b,f,b,f,b,f, close front)
1-16	passé développé – en croix (4 counts each)
1-8	4 passé relevé to pirouette position (retiré devant, close b, retiré devant, close f, etc.)
1-4	tendu front, plié port de bras forward
5-8	staying tendu front, straighten supporting leg and port de bras back
1-8	en cloche to tendu back, allongé
1-8	lift to relevé arabesque, balance

2. Rond de jambe with en cloche

1-4	4 en dehors rond de jambe
5	en cloche front
6	en cloche back
7	en cloche front
8	lower to tendu front
1-8	reverse with en dedans
1-16	repeat all

3. Rond de jambe with fondu*
* fondu - tendu with plié, close straight

1-8	fondu en croix with port de bras
1	fondu front
2	ronde de jambe to the back, straighten
3	through 1st to fondu front
4	ronde de jambe to the back, straighten
5-8	4 outside ronde de jambe close back
1-16	reverse
1-4	grand plié
5-8	relevé, lower
1-4	tendu front, plié in 4th, temps lié to tendu back
5-8	lift arabesque
1-4	balance in arabesque
5-8	close in sous-sus, plié, straighten finish

4. Rond de jambe with en cloche in 1st

1	en cloche front
2	en cloche back
3	through 1st to tendu front
4	en dehors ronde de jambe finish front
5-8	fondu in tendu front, port de bras forward and come up straightening supporting leg
1-2	en cloche back, en cloche front
3	through 1st to tendu back
4	en dedans ronde de jambe finish 1st
5-8	fondu in tendu back, port de bras back and come up straightening supporting leg
1-4	4 en dehors ronde de jambe finish front
5-8	4 en dedans rond de jambe, finish 1st
1-4	45° rond de jambe front, side, back, close 1st
5-8	45° rond de jambe back, side, front, close 1st
1-8	90° rond de jambe (grand rond de jambe en dehors) passé développé front, side, back, close 5th
1-8	90° rond de jambe (grand rond de jambe en dedans) passé développé back, side, front, close 5th
1-4	tendu back with the inside leg and full plié into allongé (toe slides back)
5-8	rise up slightly until in a lunge with front leg in plié and back leg straight and port de bras back with outside arm high in 4th
1-8	port de bras front and back again while in the lunge Continue into the splits and stretch

5. Rond de jambe

1	battement front with fondu, arm high 5th

1   battement front with fondu, arm high 5th
2   passé, straightening knee
3   développé in to arabesque, arm opens to second
4   close back
5   battement back with fondu
6,7 grand ronde de jambe to front
8   close front, straighten knee
1-8 8 outside ronde de jambe, close back
reverse

6. Rond de jambe - advanced

A   1-8   8 en dehors rond de jambe
      1-4   2 slow en dehors, arm and leg front with plié,
           straighten the supporting leg as you rond de jambe to the back
           (arm opens elongé behind the shoulder)
      5-8   in plié, rond de jambe off the floor, f, s, b, close
Reverse A
B   rond de jambe from 5th to 5th
      1-2   f, s, b, close (en dehors)
      3-4   b, s, f, close (en dedans)
      5-8   3 en dehors close back
Reverse B

7. Rond de jambe

1-2   1 outside rond de jambe to fondu tendu front
3-4   1 inside rond de jambe to the fondu tendu back
5-8   4 outside rond de jambe end front
1-2   carry to the side with fondu
3-4   port de bras to the barre
5-6   recover and straighten supporting knee
7-8   plié and lift leg à la seconde
1-2   relevé and passé
3-8   balance
1-2   move to attitude back
3-4   stretch arabesque
5-6   cloche to the front
7-8   lower leg to sous-sus, détourné
now other side
to reverse do all en dedans with an attitude front

8. Rond de jambe with temps lié

1-4   4 en dehors rond de jambe
5-6   1 slow en dehors rond de jambe with fondu (fondu with front, straighten with ronde)
7-8   through 1st to chasse front (arm high), temp lié back to tendu front
1-8   reverse
1-8   repeat en dehors (end tendu devant)
1-8   port de bras (cambré) to the front and back in tendu devant
1-32   reverse all
        (1-8 en dedans, 1-8 en dehors, 1-8 en dedans, port de bras in tendu derrière)

Rond de Jambe a terre

9. Rond de jambe – intermediate (difficult in strength)

Prepare 1 tendu front with plié, arm front, 2- arm and leg side

1-2	2 en dehors ronde de jambe
3-4	2 en dehors slightly off the floor
5-8	1 slow grand ronde de jambe, finish front
1-8	4x - brush back, passé, développé front
1-8	4x - plié in attitude front, relevé straighten both legs
1-8	balance with leg extended front
1-24	reverse all (lower from the front position brushing leg through 1st to the back to begin 1st en dedans rond de jambe)
1-6	balance in arabesque
7	sous-sus
8	plié, straighten finish

10. Advanced rond de jambe with soutenu en tournant

1-4	4 ronde de jambe en dehors

(the next 4 counts are all connected, en dehors with soutenu, en dedans with soutenu)

5	ronde de jambe in fondu f-s-b
6	pull in relevé 5th (soutenu) with ½ turn

now facing other side

7	fondu ronde de jambe b-s-f
8	pull into 5th relevé (soutenu with ½ turn) end tendu front
1-2	temps lié front, arm through 1st and up
3-4	temps lié back, arm through 1st and open 2nd
5-8	port de bras forward in fondu, straighten up and close 5th
1-2	passé, développé front with fondu
3-4	passé, développé side with fondu
5-6	passé, développé back with fondu
7-8	soutenu (closing back on relevé, no turn), and lower
1-2	passé, développé back with fondu
3-4	passé, développé side with fondu
5-6	passé, développé front with fondu
7-8	soutenu (closing front with détourné), lower

ready, other side

11. Rond de jambe with practice for renversé – notes describe R side

Part A

1-4	4 ronde de jambe en dehors
5-8	en cloche front, back, front, lower to tendu front – use port de bras
1-8	fondu and port de bras forward, straighten supporting leg and port de bras back
1-4	4 ronde de jambe en dedans
5-8	en cloche back, front, back, lower tendu
1-8	fondu in tendu back, port de bras forward and back, on 8 straighten and close back

Part B

1-2	tendu R side, close front with fondu, inside leg coupé back (arm to 1st)
3-5	step flat on L and R leg extends front (cut under) (arm to 5th) and continues grand ronde de jambe from front to back
6	arabesque turns into attitude back with tilt toward barre,
7-8	pull under to pas de bourrée en tournant to the other side

Repeat Part B on L side

Repeat Part B on both sides with the ronde de jambe on relevé

When you cut under go straight up on relevé

1. Rond de jambe a terre and en l'air

prepare:	1	tendu front with plié (arm to 1st)
	2	rond to 2nd straightening supporting leg (arm opens 2nd)
	1-4	4 en dehors rond de jambe a terre
	5-6	leg comes back to front through 1st chasse forward into tendu back, (port de bras low to high 5th)
	7-8	temps lié back to tendu front (arm through 1st open 2nd)
	1-8	reverse
	1-2	battement front, carry to the side
	3-6	4 en dehors rond de jambe en l'air
	7-8	close back
	1-8	reverse

2. Rond de jambe en l'air – face the barre

1-2	passé développé right leg side
3-4	2 en dehors rond de jambe en l'air
5,6,7	relevé, 3 en dehors rond de jambe
8	close back
1-8	same to the left, close front on 8
1-8	right again with en dedans rond de jambe, close front
1-8	left again with en dedans rond de jambe, close front

3. Rond de jambe en l'air – fouetté turn preparation

1	passé
2	développé front with plié
3-4	rond de jambe from front to side and straighten supporting leg
5,6,7	3 en dehors rond de jambe en l'air
8	close back
1-8	reverse with en dedans rond de jambe
1-16	repeat with a relevé on count 3, stay in relevé for rond de jambe

4. Rond de jambe en l'air and fondu

1-2	fondu (coupé and plié), développé front
3-4	fondu, développé side
5	relevé and touch passé back
6	touch passé front (same leg is staying in passé)
7	touch passé back
8	extend side
1-4	4 en dehors rond de jambe en l'air (still in relevé)
5-6	1 double en dehors rond de jambe
7-8	lower to tendu, close back
1-16	reverse

5. Ronde de jambe en l'air

1	battement side
2	ronde de jambe en L'air en dehors
3	double ronde de jambe en l'air en dehors
4	close
5-8	repeat with en dedans
1-2	relevé in 5th, fondu coupé back
3-4	relevé in 5th, fondu coupé front
5-6	relevé in 5th, fondu coupé back
7-8	relevé in 5th, lower 5th

Fondu, Développé and Stretches

1. <u>Simple développé en croix with 1st port de bras</u>

1	passé, arm low
2	attitude front, arm 1st
3,4	développé to full extension, arm to seconde
+	close 5th
5-8	same to the side, 1-4 to the back, 5-8 to the side
1-16	repeat with relevé

2. <u>En croix fondu - fondu = coupé plié, stretch both legs</u>

1-16	45° fondu en croix
1-16	90° fondu en croix with relevé on the extension

3. <u>Basic fondu - fondu = coupé plié, stretch both legs</u>

1-4	fondu front, 1st port de bras
5-8	fondu inside leg back, 1st port de bras
1-8	fondu side, arm high (twice as slow, working very high) close back
1-16	reverse (1-4 back, 5-8 inside leg front, 1-8 side change)
1-32	repeat with relevé on the extension

4. <u>Développé, fouetté, and penché</u>

1-16	développé en croix
1-2	développé front
3-4	fouetté to the barre ending in à la seconde keeping leg high
5-6	fouetté to arabesque, other side
7-8	plié in arabesque raising the leg and recover to straight knee
1-6	penché forward and recover
7-8	sous-sus, lower
	ready other side

5. <u>Fondu and développé</u>

1-2	coupé, passé
3-4	développé front
5	bend leg to attitude, plié
6-7	stretch développé, relevé
8	close
1-8	coupé inside leg back same to the back
1-2	fondu in coupé front, développé a l seconde relevé
3-4	fondu in coupé back, développé a l seconde relevé
5-8	fondu in coupé front, développé a l seconde relevé (slower and higher)
1-8	repeat the 3 fondu to the side (first one coupé back)

6. <u>Fondu développé</u>

1-2	passé, développé front fondu (with plié)
3-4	pull back into passé straightening supporting leg, développé back fondu
5-6	turn away from the barre to the front on the other side, straighten supporting leg
7-8	en cloche to back plié, close 5th
1-8	other side
1-2	passé, développé side fondu
3	rond de jambe to front, straighten supporting leg
4	rond de jambe to the side plié
5	rond de jambe to the back, straighten supporting leg
6-7	plié lift arabesque
8	close back finish
1-8	reverse last 8 counts

7. Fondu and passé relevé

1	brush front (45 or 90) – arm in 2nd
2	bring into fondu (coupé front in plié) – arm to first – head inclines toward barre
3	extend to the front again, straightening both legs – arm open back to 2nd – head opens
4	close
5-8	same to the side
1-4	same to the back only the arm is in arabesque, first, arabesque
5	battement side
6-7	leg comes into passé turned in both knees bent,
	then opens back through passé releasing to a high battement side.
	(swivel or "in and out ")
8	close back
1-16	reverse the whole thing
1	passé relevé
2	close back plié, arm slightly rotated back
3	passé relevé
4	close front plié, arm first
5-8	repeat last 4

8. Barre Adage

piqué	1-2	passé, développé front with plié
	3-4	piqué into arabesque
	5-6	plié in arabesque
	7-8	pas bourrée en tournant to other side
	1-8	same other side
tombé	1-2	passé with plié, développé front relevé
	3-4	tombé forward with port de bras
	5-6	push back to leg en avant
	7-8	close 5th front détourné
	1-8	same other side
piqué	1-2	balancé away from the barre
	3-4	piqué arabesque to face the barre
	5-8	change to attitude derrière, balance with arms in 5th
	1-4	hold
	5-8	close to the back turning to other side plié
	1-8	other side

9. Extension stretch
* Add on to the end of any combination. If your music is fast, each stretch may need to be 16 counts.

1-2	take the heel of your inside leg in your other hand, both legs are bent,
	stretch the leg devant straightening both legs
3-6	hold
7-8	let go trying to hold the leg up and close
1-8	same with outside leg in outside hand stretching front and carrying to à la seconde
1-8	outside leg in outside hand behind, quad stretch, knees together, foot touching derrière
1-4	knee in front to chest
5-8	carry knee to side
1-8	take knee on around to back, stretch in attitude with penché

10. Port de bras and développé fondu

1-4	full port de bras forward (cambré) and come up
5-8	développé devant with fondu and close
1-4	port de bras to the barre
5-8	développé à la seconde with fondu and close back
1-4	cambré back and recover
5-8	développé derrière with fondu and close
1-8	repeat to the side

Frappé

1. **Frappé**
   - 16   4 frappe en croix
   - 16   repeat on relevé

2. **Frappé**
   - 1-16   4 frappé each direction en croix
   - 1-8   double frappé 2 times en croix
   - 1-8   even petite battement with wrapped foot
   - 1-32   repeat in relevé with a stretched foot,
   - on last count of petite battement pull up to passé balance arms high

3. **Frappé**
   - 16   4 frappé each direction en croix
   - 16   half time, 8 double f, double b
   - 8   even petite battement with wrapped foot
   - 8   even petite battement with fully stretched foot
   - 1-8   end with foot in front, relevé balance with arms in middle 5th

4. **Frappé (prepare sur le cou de pied)**
   - 16   1 frappé en croix, 4 times
   - 16   double frappé en croix, 4 times
   - 8   petite battement with accent front (+ is in back, on the count in front)
   - 8   petite battement with accent back (+ is in front, on the count in back)
   - repeat on relevé

5. **Frappé with coupé (foot stays stretched through out exercise) - en croix**
   - 1   frappé front ouverte
   - 2   coupé F
   - 3   coupé B (inside leg)
   - 4   coupé F
   - 5   frappé out to the side
   - 6   coupé B
   - 7   coupé F (inside leg)
   - 8   coupé B
   - 1   frappé out to the back
   - 2   coupé B
   - 3   coupé F (inside leg)
   - 4   coupé B
   - 5   frappé out to the side
   - 6   coupé F
   - 7   coupé B (inside leg)
   - 8   coupé F
   - 1-16   repeat last 16
   - 1-8   petite battement with accent front (+ is in back, on the count in front)
   -          (1/2 time for beginners)
   - 1-8   petite battement with accent back (+ is in front, on the count in back)
   - 1-8   end with foot in front, relevé, draw leg up to passé and balance

6. **Frappé**
   - 1-4   3 frappé front, 1 double to the side
   - 5-8   3 frappé side, 1 double to the back
   - 1-4   3 frappé back,1 double to the side
   - 5-8   double front, double side, double back, double side
   - reverse, then repeat all on relevé

7.   Coupé with sautés = ballonné

1	tendu front ouverte
2	ronde de jambe to the back
+3	en cloche to the front with sauté, land in coupé front plié
+4	straighten to seconde with sauté, land coupé back plié
5-8	reverse 1-4
1-8	frappé 2 times en croix
1-16	½ time double frappes 2 times en croix

reverse all

8.   Frappé and battu

1-16	4 single frappé each direction en croix
1-8	double frappé 1 times en croix
	(½ time - if you can go full speed you will have 2 times en croix)
1-8	relevé battu
	arm takes four counts doing and en dehors circle, 4 counts en dedans

repeat all on relevé with stretched foot

9.   Frappé and body facings

1-4	4 frappé front
5-8	4 frappé side
1-4	4 frappé back
5-8	4 double frappé side
1-2	relevé and touch ankle cou de pied back, cou de pied front, point tendu front in plié facing out from the barre
3-4	relevé, touch front, back, point tendu back in plié facing into the barre
5-8	repeat last 4
1-8	relevé petite battement for 7 on 8 lower with sur le cou de pied back
1-32	reverse all except instead of lowering on last count, wrap foot and balance

10.   Frappé with petit passé

1-2	pick up to coupé
3-4	close 5th back in plié, arm in 2nd rolls back with palm up, head out
5-6	coupé
7-8	close 5th front in plié, arm rolls forward in 2nd palm down, looking in palm
1-8	repeat
1-16	4 frappe each direction en croix
1-16	doubles ½ time en croix
1-16	relevé battu, arm en bas

relevé and balance with wrapped foot

11.   Frappé with relevé and plié

1-3	3 frappé devant
4	double frappe derrière
5-7	3 frappé derrière
8	double frappe devant
1-3	3 frappé à la seconde
4	double à la seconde
5-8	4 doubles à la seconde - relevé with the cou de pied, plié on the opening

reverse

12.   Frappé with relevés

1-4	4 frappé devant (do not close last one)
5-8	4 demi relevés with the leg extended devant
1-24	continue en croix
1-16	double frappé en croix - 2x
1-16	16 counts of petite battement, relevé on second 8
1-8	balance with a wrapped sur le cou de pied

Grand Battement

Most of these combinations should be done twice for an intermediate student.
You might repeat with relevé, then détourné and do other side flat and with relevé,
Or you could do Right side, détourné, Left side, détourné, and then a second time in relevé.

1. **Grand battement en croix**
   - 1-4 2 grand battement
   - 5-6 battement with développé close (passé, stretch, close)
   - 7-8 battement with retiré close (battement, pull in to passé, close)

2. **Grand battement en croix**
   - 1-8 1 slow développé
   - 1-8 4 grand battement

3. **Grand battement en croix**
   - 1-4 2 grand battement
   - 5-8 battement out, 6-lower to tendu, 7- lift to battement again, 8- close

4. **Grand battement en croix**
   - 1-4 2 grand battement
   - 5   battement out
   - 6   pull into passé
   - 7   développé
   - 8   close

5. **Grand battement en croix**
   - 1-4   2 slow grand battement
   - +5+6+7,8   3 quick battement last one closing plié

6. **Développé and grand battement - en croix**
   - 1-4 passé(1), développé(2-3), close(4)
   - 5-8 2 grand battement

7. **Everybody's favorite grand battement**
   - 1-4 2 battement front
   - 5-8 battement front, cloche back, cloche front, close front
   - 1-4 2 battement side
   - 5-8 battement side, in and out, close back*
   - 1-4 2 battement back
   - 5-8 battement back, cloche front, cloche back, close back
   - 1-4 2 battement side
   - 5-8 battement side, in and out*, close front
     * from the battement side the leg is pulled into a turned-in passé with the standing leg in plié, then the passé turns out and the leg extends out to the side again as the supporting leg straightens.

8. **Grand battement en croix second time in relevé**
   - 1-6 3 grand battement
   - 7-8 demi plié

9. **Grand battement with port de bras**
   - 1-6 3 grand battement front
   - 7-8 port de bras forward and come up arm will end high 5th
   - 1-6 3 grand battement side (arm will open on 1st grand battement)
   - 7-8 port de bras to the barre and open
   - 1-6 3 grand battement back (arm in arabesque)
   - 7-8 arm reaches side and continues back with back port de bras and come up arm high
   - 1-6 3 grand battement side (arm opening on 1st battement)
   - 7-8 détourné

Grand Battement

10. Grand battement with lunge

front	1-2	grand battement front, cloche through to tendu back plié
	3-4	repeat 1-2
	5-6	battement front, lower to tendu front plié
	7-8	battement front, close 5th
side	1-4	2 battement changing to the side
	5-8	battement side, pull into passé plié turned in, back out to battement, close
back	1-2	grand battement back, lower to tendu front plié
	3-4	repeat 1-2
	5-6	battement back, lower to tendu back plié
	7-8	battement back, close 5th
side	1-8	repeat side

11. Frappé and grand battement - Prepare - sur le cou de pied
En croix - arm high 5th for front and back, arm in seconde for side

1-2	1 frappé to sur le cou de pied
3-4	1 frappé to 5th
5-8	2 grand battement
1-24	continue en croix

12. Battement soutenu relevé

1	battement front with plié
2	soutenu (as the leg lowers rise to demi-pointe closing 5th)
3	battement back with plié (inside leg)
4	soutenu
5	battement side with plié
6	close back 5th relevé
7-8	demi-plié, sous-sus
1-2	battement back with plié, soutenu relevé
3-4	battement front with plié, soutenu relevé (inside leg)
5-6	battement side with plié, soutenu relevé changing
7-8	détourné and lower

13. Battement and en cloche

1-4	2 battement devant
5-8	2 battement à la seconde
1-4	2 battement derrière
5-8	en cloche to the back, front, back, close
1-16	now reverse

14. Battement and en cloche

1-8	En Cloche in attitude f,b,f,b,f,b,f. close
1-8	2 grand battement side, 1 battement with in and out to the side
1-8	4 battement front
1-8	3 battement side closing f,b,f. Close the 3rd in plié and passé relevé from front to back.
1-32	reverse all

15. Grand battement and passé

1-4	2 grand battement devant
5-8	1 relevé passé over (inside leg)
1-4	2 grand battement devant (inside leg)
5-8	relevé passé over (outside leg)
1-4	2 grand battement derriere
5-8	1 relevé passé under
1-4	2 grand battement derriere
5-8	1 relevé passé under

Barre Extras

1. Barre pirouette

1-2	passé with arm high, close back in plié arm open seconde rotated back
3-4	passé with arm high, close front arm to first
5-8	tendu side, prepare fourth back with plié, en dehors pirouette, close back
1-4	reverse 1-4 (passé to the front, passé close back)
5-8	tendu side, leg to fourth back, barre arm to the front, en dedans pirouette, close front

2. Back to the barre – in 1st - cabriole preparation (if you have strong barres)

1	battement front
2	lower to tendu front plié
3	battement front leg, also kicking supporting leg up to beat top leg
4	land plié tendu front, close
5-8	continue other side

3. Piqués and pirouettes - face barre, R coupé back

1-2	piqué R (L coupé back), come down in plié (L still in coupé)
3-4	piqué L (R coupé back), plié in coupé
5-6	piqué R (L passé), 4th back plié
7-8	en dehors pirouette finish back
1-8	continue other side

4. Passé développé - face barre in first

1	R passé
2	turn passé in across body
3-4	turn passé out
5-7	développé side
8	close 1st
1-8	Left side
1	tendu R back
2-4	lift to arabesque
5-6	plié in arabesque
7-8	straighten closing 1st
1-8	Left side

5. Exercise for batterie – face the barre in 5th

Part A - right side

1+	tendu side ouverte
2	flex the foot and close it to 3rd in back without putting weight on it
+	now barely open it to the side and place it in front 3rd

this should simulate the way legs fit together in beats

3+	tendu side
4+	beat front, back
5+	tendu side
6+7+	beat back, front, back, front,
8	beat to the back and put weight on both feet
1-8	part A – left side

Part B - right side

1+	tendu side
2+3+4+	beat b,f,b,f,b,f
5	tendu side
6	plié in 2nd
7	temps lie to tendu L side
8	close L front
1-8	part B – left side

Port de Bras

> **** Definition - Port de bras ****
> The difference between a port de bras and an adage is somewhat blurred. If the exercise is mostly a simple moving of the arms and small leg movements, I call it a port de bras. An adage is more advanced and works on the épaulement, developing extension, strength and balance.

> ****Teaching Tip ****
> To develop good arms it is important to start with plain port de bras (just arms movements). An exercise like #1 is very beneficial in beginning classes. Let your students master simple arm movements before adding leg movements.

1. **Just port de bras, begin croisé, R front to C2**

1-8	first port de bras
	1-2 arms from low to first position
	3-4 arms open seconde and head moves to the R
	5-6 wrists lift and palms turn down (if you teach this way)
	It is also good beginning technique to keep the curved arm and begin lowering.
	7-8 finish lowering to low fifth, eyes down
1-8	repeat
1-16	2x port de bras en dehors through high 5th (first, fifth, seconde, en bas)
1-16	2x port de bras en dedans through high 5th (seconde, fifth, first, en bas)

2. **My favorite beginning port de bras, begin croisé, R front to C2**

1-8	first port de bras
	1-2 arms from low to first position
	3-4 arms open seconde and head moves to the R
	5-6 wrists lift and palms turn down (if you teach this way)
	It is also good beginning technique to keep the curved arm and begin lowering.
	7-8 finish lowering to low fifth, eyes down
1-8	repeat
1-16	2x port de bras en dehors through high 5th
1-8	développé R croisé devant to C2
1-8	développé R à la seconde en face, and close back
1-8	développé R into arabesque to C1, and close back
1-8	1-4 demi plié arms breathe, 5-8 wait

   * This is the part I find most helpful. Kids usually turn to much to the side wall for their diagonal positions. When we are doing the demi plié, I am having them look to see that the space in their legs is making a diamond in the mirror. Now other side.

3. **Port de bras, croisé, R front to C2**

1-4	down stage arm inside circle port de bras (up the side to high 5th, down the front)
5-8	upstage arm inside circle port de bras
1-2	tombé forward (arms through 1st to 2nd)
3-4	port de bras forward in lunge (arms lower)
5-7	port de bras back in lunge (arms high 5th), recover to tendu back (arms open 2nd)
8	close fifth (arms low)

4. **3 body facings, croisé, R front to C2**

1-2	tendu croisé devant, close changing to en face
3-4	tendu en face devant, close changing to effacé
5	tendu effacé devant
6-7	en cloche back to 2nd arabesque (arms will go through 1st to 2nd arabesque)
8	close, ready other side

   * variation - close tendu with plié, when closing plié change to the next direction.

** To practice all the body facings see page 35.

Adage

1. **Port de bras, penché and promenade, croisé, R front to C2**
1-8	2x first port de bras, head opening to audience
1-8	2x en dehors port de bras through high 5th, head opening to audience
1-4	tendu croisé devant, temps lie through to tendu back, close
5-8	tendu croisé derrière, temps lie back to tendu front, close
1-8	repeat last 8 (stay in tendu front, don't close on 8)
1-8	en cloche through to arabesque, penché
1-8	promenade (en dedans) to C1, close back, plié, sous-sus

   other side

2. **3 body facings and arabesque promenade, croisé, R front to C2**
1	tendu croisé devant
2	temp lié though 4th
3	tendu croisé derrière
4	close back plié 5th
5	tendu écarté devant
6	pivot and temp lié though 4th changing to C1
7-8	lift first arabesque
1-5	promenade to the right (complete circle back to same corner)
6	plié lift the arabesque
7+8	pas de bourrée b, s, f ready other side

3. **3 body facings and arabesque, croisé, R front to C2**
1-2	tendu croisé devant, close
3	tendu écarté devant, don't close
4	pivot to effacé devant to C1
5	en cloche back into arabesque (arms through 1st to change to Russian 3rd arabesque)
6-7	hold arabesque
8	close en face
1-8	4 tendu à la seconde closing back - now other side

4. **Développé in 3 body facings, croisé, R front to C2**
1-4	développé croisé devant and close
5-8	turn en face and développé R à la seconde, close R in front changing to C1
1-4	développé effacé
5-8	tombé, pas de bourrée (b,s,f) now L is in front ready for other side

5. **Développés, promenade and lunge, croisé, R front to C2**
1-4	first port de bras
5-8	en dehors port de bras through high 5th
1-4	développé croisé devant
5-8	développé side écarté devant (close back)
1-4	développé back 1st arabesque
5-8	promenade to the left to C2 changing arms to 2nd arabesque
1-4	lower to plié tendu back lunge, port de bras forward and back
5-7	pull up to relevé 5th with high arms
8	lower, open arms, ready for other side

6. Développés, promenade and penché, croisé, R front to C2

1-4	développé front
5-8	développé side, close back
1-4	développé back into first arabesque
5-8	promenade to the left from C2 to C1, changing arms from 1st to 2nd arabesque
1-2	balancé R and L
3-4	piqué 1st arabesque on R to C1, lower to flat in arabesque
5-7	small penché
8	L leg goes en cloche to the tendu front, close

reverse

7. Développés and arabesque, croisé, R front to C2

1-4	R leg passé, développé <u>first arabesque</u>, close
5-8	L leg passé développé <u>effacé devant</u>, (R arm high), close
1-4	R passé développé side, <u>écarté devant</u>, close front
1-2	chassé to C1 (R arm to 5th, coming down through first)
3-4	into first arabesque,
5-6	plié in arabesque
7+8	pas de bourrée b,s,f

ready other side

8. 3 Arabesques, prepare in 5th en face, arms in 1st

These arabesques are held for a long time so the student can gain strength and height.

1-2	plié and chasse to stage right into 1st arabesque
3-4	staying in arabesque rotate arms into 2nd arabesque (front arm goes up, back arm down)
5-6	holding arabesque move arms to 3rd arabesque (Cecchetti 3rd arabesque, both arms forward, upstage arm 45 up)
7-8	turning en face, lower to tendu side, arms 5th
8	close 5th, arms 1st
1-8	same to the left

9. Intermediate adage, croisé, R front to C2

1	tendu croisé devant, arms in 3rd (left arm front, right arm in seconde)
2	temp lié
3	tendu croisé derriere (left arm straightens to arabesque line)
4	pivot to tendu front to C4 (right arm front in 3rd)(back to audience)
5	temp lié
6	tendu back right arm front in arabesque
7	pivot back to tendu front to C2
8	close 5th
1	tendu R leg side to écarté
2	pivot to tendu front effacé
3	brush R leg through to tendu back (left arm comes down to arabesque)
4	close 5th back
5	tendu R to the side en face
6	close 5th front plié prepare
7-8	en dehors pirouette finish back

10. Adage begin in 2nd en face

1-4	grand plié
5-8	demi plié, pivot in plié to wall 5, straighten into 1st <u>arabesque</u>
1-4	promenade R to C2 changing arms to <u>2nd arabesque</u>
5	pull back leg into passé (arms 1st)
6-7	développé <u>écarté derrière</u>
8	lower to 2nd en face, ready for other side

Adage

11. Adagio with fondu and développé, begin croisé in 5th

1-4 fondu in coupé, arms low and stretch into développé croisé devant (don't close)
5-8 fondu in coupé, stretch and développé écarté devant (don't close)
1-4 fondu in coupé derriere and stretch into first arabesque
5-8 back leg failli forward into coupé fondu and pas de bourrée (en tournant optional)
(with each fondu the arms circle en dehors to their position)

12. Développés with promenade and pirouette – prepare in 5th en face

1-6 développé a la quatrième devant, arms through 1st to 5th
7-8 close 5th arms open
1-6 développé à la seconde, arms though 1st to 5th
7-8 holding leg height in 2nd, turn toward SL into 1st arabesque (fouetté)
1-4 promenade to the left changing into attitude, ending at C1 attitude croisé derrière
5-6 stretch fondu into 2nd arabesque
7-8 pas de bourrée b, s, f – en face
1-2 pas de bourrée b, s, f into 4th preparation croisé
3-6 En dehors pirouette finish croisé lunge
7-8 straighten to tendu croisé derrière, close 5th en face

13. Advanced adage – croisé, R front to C2

1-2 passé
3-4 développé R croisé devant, fondu, arms 1st
5-6 piqué devant into attitude croisé derrière
7-8 stretch into arabesque (Russian 3rd arabesque)
1 close 5th en face
2 passé R
3-4 développé à la seconde
5-8 fondu (5) piqué to side to other à la seconde, fondu and lift
1-2 promenade into arabesque
3-6 penché
7-8 stretch arabesque
1-2 fondu in arabesque
3-4 pull under pas de bourrée to fourth
5-8 en dedans pirouette, close back, ready other side

1. <u>**Center tendu**</u>
    8 tendu side en arrière, with outward port de bras
    8 tendu side en avant, with inward port de bras
    or
    8 tendu side en avant, head tilts toward the working leg, arms in 2nd
    8 tendu side en arrière, head tilts away from the working leg, arms in 5th
    (teaching the head to move with the foot that closes front)
    * this exercise can also be done with grand battement

2. <u>**Tendu and sautés**</u>
1-4	2 tendu side en avant
5-8	3rd tendu with plié and lean toward tendu leg with arms in seconde leaning, close
1-4	4 changement
5-8	4 count sous-sus
1-16	other side
1-32	reverse

3. <u>**Tendu with body positions -**</u> begin croisé
1-8	2 tendu devant, 2 tendu derrière
1 -2	1 tendu croisé devant
3-4	1 a la quatrième devant (arms in 2nd) en face
5	1 tendu efface devant C1, don't close (front arm high-shaded)
6	cloche to tendu back (arms 2nd arabesque)
7-8	lower to a small 4th plié, passé relevé, close back

    other side then reverse with derrière positions
    * passé relevé can be en dehors pirouette

4. <u>**Tendu and en dehors pirouette from 5th**</u> - En face R foot front
1-2	tendu L side, close front
+3+4	2 dégagé L side, close back, front
5,6	tendu R side, close front
+7+8	2 dégagé R side, close back, front
1	plié
2	passé relevé
3	close plié without changing
4	straight knees
5	plié
6,7	en dehors pirouette, close back
8	straighten
1-16	reverse

    * after this is done well, change the second 8 counts to:
1	plié
2,3	en dehors pirouette, close front
4,5	en dehors pirouette, close front
6,7	en dehors pirouette, close back
8	straighten

5. <u>**Center tendu – begin croisé R foot front to corner 2**</u>
1	tendu croisé devant
2-3	temps lié to tendu back – downstage arm high looking under
4-5	temps lié to tendu front
6-7	ronde from front to side changing to corner 1- écarté devant
8	close back
1-8	left leg does 4 tendu to the side (écarté derrière)
	closing 1st , 5th back, 1st, 5th front, arms do first port de bras
1-2	step L sous-sus to C2, left arm high in 3rd, plié 5th, L arm to 1st
3-4	step R sous-sus to C1, right arm high in 3rd, plié with L coupé back, R arm to 1st
5-6	pas de bourrée en tournant 7-8 demi plié prepare for other side

Center Tendu

6. **Center tendu with en dehors pirouettes (or just passé relevé)**

1-4	2 tendu croisé devant (arms in mid 3rd, upstage arm front)
5-8	2 tendu croisé derrière (arms switch)
1-4	2 tendu croisé devant (arms high 3rd, upstage arm high)
5-8	2 tendu croisé derrière (arms switch)
1-8	4 tendu en face à la seconde (en arrière) ~~moving back~~

Pirouette preparation section

1	tendu side
2	place foot in 4th in back plié
3	passé relevé, or en dehors pirouette
4	close 5th back
5-8	other side
1-8	repeat
1-4	2 tendu en face à la seconde en avant
5-8	1 tendu écarté devant

7. **The cut-in-half combination – en face R foot front**

1-4	4 tendu R devant
5-8	4 tendu L derrière
1-4	4 tendu R à la seconde (all changing)
5-8	4 tendu L à la seconde (all changing)
1-2	2 tendu devant
3-4	2 tendu derrière
5-6	2 tendu R à la seconde changée
7-8	2 tendu L à la seconde changée
1	1 tendu devant
2	1 tendu derrière
3	1 tendu R side changée
4	1 tendu L side changée
5-8	tendu R side, plié in 2nd, tendu L side, close front

other side

8. **Simple tendu to learn to reverse**

1-4	4 tendu devant
5-8	4 tendu derrière
1-4	4 tendu under (à la seconde moving en arrière)
5-8	tendu R side, close 4th back prepare, en dehors pirouette close back
1-16	repeat other side

now reverse

1-4	4 tendu derrière
5-8	4 tendu devant
1-4	4 tendu over (à la seconde moving en avant)
5-8	tendu R devant, lower to prepare, en dedans pirouette, close front
1-16	repeat other side

9. **Tendu à la seconde with port de bras side**

1	tendu R à la seconde, arms through 1st to 2nd
2	port de bras to the side away from the leg
3	recover to upright, arms though 1st to 2nd
4	close 5th derrière, arms low
5-8	other side
1-8	repeat
1-16	reverse with tendu moving en avant and port de bras toward the leg

Cecchetti Body Facings

Croisé aevant

À la quatrième devant

Écarté devant

Effacé devant

À la seconde

Épaulé

À la quatrième derrière

Croisé derrière

Cecchetti Body Facings

Teach the Cecchetti positions in this order and they flow clockwise in a nice pattern.

1. 4 slow tendu in each position. Close 4th tendu in plié while moving to the next direction.
   (it is good to start with 4 to get a feel for each épaulement and have time to think where they are gong next)
2. 2 tendu each position.
3. 1 or 2 développés each direction
4. 2 tendu and 1 développé

Pas de Bourrée

There are 4 basic pas de bourrée.
Any of them can begin with either - fondu in sur le cou de pied front or back
                              or - fondu with a dégagé side.
Any of them can commence with the front or back foot.

1. Pas de bourrée dessous: step back, side, front (under)
2. Pas de bourrée dessus: step front, side, back (over)
3. Pas de bourrée devant: step front, side, front
4. Pas de bourrée derrière: step back, side, back

The pas de bourrée exercise - do combinations A - D as one exercise

Pas de bourrée is meant to be done in three counts. For this technique drill I like to do it in 4 counts to
ensure the accuracy of their positions. Later the counts 1,2,3,4 should be changed to + 1, 2, 3.
All of these pas de bourrée are in fondu on count 1, on pointe or demi-pointe on counts 2 and 3, and flat
moving into the next fondu on 4.

A. 4 Pas de bourrée under (with cou de pied, commencing from the back)
    1   fondu with L sur le cou de pied back
    2   step back
    3   side
    4   front (closing 5th and lowering to demi plié)
    5-8   other side
    1-8   repeat

B. 4 Pas de bourrée over (with cou de pied, commencing from the front)
    1   fondu with R sur le cou de pied front
    2   step front
    3   side
    4   back (closing 5th and lowering to demi plié)
    5-8   other side
    1-8   repeat

C. Under, over, under, over (with degage side and the leg will always switch on 1-2)
    commencing from the front
    1   fondu with R degage side
    2   step back
    3   side
    4   front (closing 5th and lowering to demi plié)
    commencing from the back
    5   fondu with L degage side
    6   step front
    7   side
    8   back (closing 5th and lowering to demi plié)
    1-8   repeat last 8

D. 4 Pas de bourrée under en tournant (2 half turns – 2 whole turns)
    1   coupé L with fondu
    2   step back turning to the L upstage
    3   step R behind facing upstage
    4   step L front in 5th
    5   coupé R back with fondu
    6   step back turning to the R into en face
    7   step L behind
    8   step R 5th front en face
    1-8   repeat turning a complete turn with each pas de bourrée

1. **En dehors technique**
    * *prepare arms to first and open L arm so arms are in 3rd*
    1   tendu R to the side, arms open 2nd
    2   place R in 4th position back plié, R arm moves down and to the front
    3-4   relevé on L (R to retiré front), L arm closes 1st, close back
    * this exercise should be done just balancing in passé before adding the turn
    * this will alternate sides
    * if you do the above preparation and close front, you will continue on same side and could
       do ¼ turns in sequence or ½ turns

2. **En dedans basic pirouette technique**
    1   tendu front – arms in 2nd
    2   lunge forward (front leg plié, back leg straight),arms to 3rd (same arm and leg front)
    3   en dehors pirouette (arms to 1st or 5th)
    4   close front
    continue alternating sides

3. **En dehors**
    1+a2   tombé R, pas de bourrée back, side, front (L,R,L)
    3+a4   tombé L, pas de bourrée back, side, front (R,L,R)
    5-6   tendu R prepare 4th back
    7-8   en dehors pirouette finish back, other side
    *variation - same combination only finish the pirouette croisé derrière lunge

4. **Center turns**
    1,2   step L plié relevé développé R à la seconde, close front plié
    3,4   relevé développé L à la seconde, lower to 2nd plié
    5,6   push to passé relevé on L leg, lower R passé to coupé back plié,
    7,8   pas de bourrée to fourth
    1-8   en dedans close front, en dehors close front, piqué R, lame duck R

5. **Center développé with en dedans - 5th R foot back**
    1,2   glissade R (no change), développé R à la seconde close front,
    3,4   glissade L (no change), développé L à la seconde close front
    5,6   glissade R (no change), développé R à la seconde,
    7   tombé the R across to croisé 4th lunge,
    8   en dedans pirouette finish back

6. **En dehors, pas de bourrée, en dedans**
    1-4   tendu side, 4th back plié prepare, en dehors pirouette, finish coupé back
    5-6   pas de bourrée en tournant to croisé
    7-8   en dedans pirouette finish enface close front

7. **Varied preparations moving forward prepare in 5th with R in front**
    1-4   chassé forward, pas de bourrée to 5th L in front
    5-8   en dehors pirouette close back
    1-4   tombé forward, pas de bourrée to 5th R front
    5-8   en dehors pirouette close back
    1-4   piqué forward, pas de bourrée to 5th L in front
    5-8   en dehors pirouette close back
    1-4   tendu left front (arms in second), tombé forward (left arm forward)
    5-8   en dedans pirouette

8. **Balancé, retiré balance and en dehors**   (waltz each count is 3, with a 4/4 each count is 2)
    1-2   balancé R, piqué L with R in retiré front and balance
            (arms swing R middle 3rd, L middle 3rd)
    3-4   repeat
    5-6   repeat but don't hold the retiré and put R down in back in small 4th
    7-8   en dehors pirouette finish back and continue alternating sides

Petite Allegro 2/4

Most of these combinations are designed to do the second side without stopping.
Unless specified all of the petite allegros begin in 5th with R devant.
(Most of the combinations end with L devant to begin other side.)

Glissade: Unless specified glissade will be *glissade derrière* which moves to the side commencing with the back foot and closing front.
Pas de Chat: Unless specified the pas de chat should commence with the back foot and close front.
Jeté: Unless specified jeté will be *jeté dessus.* (jeté over) The back foot will brush in a frappé à la seconde, spring off the floor, land on that foot with the other foot in coupé back.

1. **Simple sauté - first position**
1-12	3X- plié, straight, relevé, flat
13-16	3 jumps in first, straighten

2. **Changement – beginning**
    Use the plié hold as a time to check on heels down, turn-out, and alignment.
1-3	3 changement
4	hold in plié
5-7	3 changement
8	Hold in plié
1-7	7 changement
8	hold in plié

    *for intermediate use croisé épaulement on each of the hold counts

3. **Sauté - first position**
1-4	4 sauté in first
5-7	relevé hold
8	plié
1-4	4 sauté in first
5-7	relevé hold
8	close fifth
1-4	2 échappé sauté
5-8	4 changement
1-4	2 échappé sauté
5-7	3 changement
8	soubresaut

4. **Changement with entrechat quatre**
1-8	4 changement, entrechat quatre, changement, entrechat quatre, soubresaut

5. **Changement and entrechat quatre**
    16 changement, 15 entrechat quatre, 1 royale
    *the intermediate student could use épaulement and make each jump slightly croisé

6. **Beat exercise - first position**
1-8	4 sauté in first, 4 sauté in 2nd
1-4	4 changement
5+6+	2nd, beat R in front, land 2nd, beat R in front
7+8	2nd, beat R in front, land 5th R in back

7. **Échappé battu**
1	sauté to 2nd
2	beat R devant, land 5th R derrière
3	sauté to 2nd
4	beat L devant, land 5th L derrière
5-8	4 changement

8. <u>Échappé battu with pas de bourrée</u>

1	sauté to 2nd
2	beat R devant, land 5th R derrière
3	sauté to 2nd
4	beat L devant, land 5th L derrière
5	sauté to 2nd
6	beat R devant, land on L with R coupé derrière (like entrechat trios)
7+8	pas de bourrée (back, side, back)

Or - pas de bourrée back, side, front and link it to another combination before the other side.

9. <u>Sautés</u>

1-4	2nd, 5th, 2nd, 5th
5-8	4 changement
1	2nd
2	L coupé back
3	2nd
4	R coupé back
5-8	3 jeté over, 1 assemblé over

other side   * to reverse coupé front and jeté under

10. <u>Échappé – do this en face first to make sure of placement in 4th</u>

1+	échappé 4th, fermé	2+	échappé 2nd, fermé
3+	échappé 4th fermé	4+	sous-sus, plié

11. <u>Échappé - begin in fifth croisé</u>

1+	échappé 4th, fermé
2+	échappé 2nd en face, fermé
3+	échappé 4th (other corner) croisé, fermé
4+	sous-sus, plié

11a. <u>Échappé - begin in fifth croisé</u>

1-2	échappé 4th, fermé
3-4	échappé 2nd en face, fermé
5	échappé 4th don't close
6-8	en dehors pirouette close back

12. <u>Échappé - begin in fifth croisé</u>

1-2	2 changement
3-4	échappé 4th, fermé
5-6	2 changement en face
7-8	échappé 2nd en face, fermé continue other side

13. <u>Échappé with a beat – en face R front in 5th</u>

1+2	échappé to 2nd, beat R n front close R derrière in 5th
3+4	échappé to 2nd, beat L in front close L derrière in 5th
5-8	3 changement, soubresaut

14. <u>Sauté, changement, and entrechat quatre</u>

1-8	7 sautés in 1st, sauté to 5th on 8
1-8	4 changement, 2 échappé
1-4	4 sous-sus with plié in between
5-8	2 entrechat quatre for beginners, or 4

15. <u>Changement, coupés, and assemblé</u>

1,2	2 changement
3	entrechat trois to the coupé back
+a4	pas de bourrée b,s,f
5,6	2 changement
7	entrechat trois to the coupé front
+a8	pas de bourrée f,s,b
1,2	sauté to coupé front, sauté to coupé back (other foot)
3+a4	cut assemblé (put the back coupé down and assemblé from front to back)
5-8	4 changement

Petite Allegro 6/8

1. My first glissade – L foot front in 5th
    1-3   3 glissades to the R (all closing front 5th)
    4   changement
    5-7   3 glissades to the L
    8   changement

2. Glissade with épaulement
    1-3   3 glissade to the right closing left front, left back, left front
            (tilt the head toward the front foot with a slight shouldering)
    4   sous-sus
    5-8   3 glissade to the left, closing right front, right back, right front, sous-sus

3. Glissade and easy entrechat quatre
    1   glissade en avant   (moving forward)
    2   glissade en arrière   (moving back)
    3   glissade under   (to the side, commence with front foot, close front)
    4   entrechat quatre

4. My first jeté – leave arms en bas
    1-3   3 jeté over (R, L, R)
    4   hold in the plié, L is cou de pied back, see the diamond between the knees
    5-7   3 jeté over (L, R, L)
    8   put R foot down behind in fifth
    1-3   3 jeté under (L, R, L)
    4   hold in plié, R will be cou de pied front
    5-7   3 jeté under (R, L, R)
    8   put L down in front in fifth
This does not change sides

5. My first assemblé – arms en bas
    1-3   3 assemblé over (R, L, R)
    4   stretch the knees and plié again
    5-7   3 assemblé over (L, R, L)
    8   stretch the knees and plié again
    1-3   3 assemblé under (L, R, L)
    4   stretch the knees and plié again
    5-7   3 jeté under (R, L, R)
    8   stretch the knees and plié again
This does not change sides

6. The classic jeté
    1-4   jeté R, temps levé on right, jeté L, temps levé on left
    5-8   jeté R, jeté L, jeté R, temp levé
Ready for other side

7. The classic pattern with assemblé dessus
Assemblé dessus= assemblé over = working leg goes to the seconde moving downstage
    1   assemblé (R from b to f)
    2   soubresaut (This soubresaut is just a jump upward in fifth.)
    3   assemblé (L from b to f)
    4   soubresaut
    5-8   3 assemblés (R, L, R), soubresaut
Continue other side

8. The classic pattern with assemblé dessous
Assemblé dessous= assemblé under = working leg goes to the seconde moving upstage

1	assemblé (R from f to b)
2	soubresaut (This soubresaut is just a jump upward in fifth, temps levé from 2 feet.)
3	assemblé (L from f to b)
4	soubresaut
5-8	3 assemblés (R,L,R), soubresaut

Continue other side

9. The classic pattern with assemblé en avant
Assemblé en avant = assemblé forward = working leg goes to the fourth in front moving downstage. This exercise should always have a croisé épaulement. The assemblés will move down the diagonal and every changement will change corners.

1	assemblé (R from f to f)
2	changement (change corners)
3	assemblé (L from f to f)
4	changement
5-8	3 assemblés (R,R,R), changement

10. Building on the classic, R foot back 5th
1-2	glissade derrière, jeté over (to the R)
3-4	glissade derrière, jeté over (to the L)
5-8	glissade derrière, jeté over, 2 temps levés (to the R)
1-8	repeat starting to the left
1-2	glissade derrière, assemblé over R
3-4	glissade derrière, assemblé over L
5-8	glissade derrière, 2 pas de chat derrière, royale
1-8	to the other side

* intermediate students may add beats to the jeté and assemblé

11. Glissade jeté (right foot back)
1-4	glissade jeté R, glissade jeté L
5-8	glissade R, assemblé over R, 2 entrechat quatre
	(a beginning student may just do 1 entrechat)

12. Technique glissades that close in a good 5th
to the right	1-4	3 glissades, 1 jeté
to the left	5-8	3 glissades, 1 jeté
to the right	1-4	glissade, 2 pas de chat, pas de bourrée
to the left	5-8	glissade, 2 pas de chat, pas de bourrée

13. Pas de chat
1-3	3 pas de chat to the right (arms in 3rd with R arm front)
4	changement (arms low)
5-8	same to the Left
1-2	pas de chat R, changement
3-4	pas de chat L, changement
5-6	tombé R, pas de bourrée to 4th position preparation
7-8	en dehors turn (If you close front you are ready to do the other side, or you can finish croisé lunge)

14. Assemblé
1-2	2 assemblé en avant
3+ a 4	jeté, pas de bourrée under
5-7	3 pas de chat (all toward the back foot closing front)
8	tendu a ala seconde from back to front

Petite Allegro 6/8

15. **Allegro with épaulement, begin croisé to C2**
- 1,2   sauté to the R coupé front, sauté to the L coupé back
- 3,4   cut (put L down) assemblé en arrière changing to C1
- 5   glissade derrière toward back corner
  - (glissade to the side commencing with back foot, close front)
- 6,7,8   3 entrechat quatre

16. **Changement and sissonne**
- 1-4   4 changement
- 5-6   sissonne ouverte de côté to the R, pas de bourrée
- 7-8   sissonne fermé front

17. **Sissonne effacé en avant** (start to the back of the room as it moves forward)
- 1-4   2 sissonne en avant fermé (R front toward C1)
- 5-6   sissonne en avant ouverte
- 7-8   pas de bourrée changing épaulement to other side
  - now toward left corner

* It is also beneficial to do this combination en face to check that the arabesque is straight behind.

18. **Sissonne (over, front and back)**
- 1-2   tombé pas de bourrée to the R
- 3-4   2 sissonne de côté fermé over (to the L, closing R front, then R closing L front)
- 5-8   1-4 to the other side
- 1-4   1-4 again
- 5-8   sissonne front, sissonne back change, changement

19. **Jeté, assemblé and ballonné**
- 1-4   glissade R, jeté R, glissade L, assemblé L over
- 5-6   coupé the R which is back, step on it, left leg ballonné à la seconde
- 7-8   put L down in back, assemblé under

20. **Petite allegro, prepare with R in back either in 5th or B+**
- 1,2   jeté, temp levé   (en face)
- 3,4   jeté, jeté
- 5   step plié on L, R foot coupé front (effacé to C1)
- 6,7,8   ballonné front, front, side
- 1,2   pas de bourrée (back, side, front) en face
- 3,4   2 pas de chat L, close front
- 5-8   entrechat, royale, entrechat, royale

21. **Varied combination**
- 1-2   glissade, jeté to the right
- 3,4   glissade, jeté to the left
- 5,6   pas de chat R, pas de bourrée
- 7,8   2 changement
- 1,2   glissade L, jeté L
- 3,4   coupé (cut R under), ballonné L à la seconde
- 5,6   pas de bourrée
- 7,8   entrechat, changement

22. **Sautés and pirouettes**
- 1-2   2 changement
- 3-4   sous-sus
- 5-6   entrechat quatre
- 7-8   2 changement
- 1-2   sous-sus
- 3   entrechat trois
- +a4   pas de bourrée to 4th
- 5-8   en dehors pirouette closing front

23. Glissade, jeté and sissonne (R foot back in 5th)

1-2	glissade jeté R
3-4	glissade jeté L
5-6	glissade jeté R
7-8	pas de bourrée en tournant (end in 5th L front)
1-2	sissonne changé fermé to C1 (arms in first arabesque)
3-4	sissonne fermé to C1
5-6	sissonne changé ouverte into 2nd arabesque, (windmill arms) (front arm goes up and around, back arm down to front)
7-8	chassé back, assemblé half turn (around to the front again) close L back to be ready for the other side

24. Sauté arabesques

1-2	chasse R (toward stage R), sauté in 1st arabesque on R,
3-4	step forward to sauté on L with R coupé back, (R arm high in 3rd) head to the L
4	brush back to sauté in same 1st arabesque again
5-8	chasse L (toward SL), sauté arabesque on L, R comes front to do soutenu L
1-8	other side

25. Ballonné and ballotté

en face

1-2	2 changement
3-4	glissade L, assemblé over
5-6	step L front pose (a gentle piqué forward into a low arabesque, arms forward to an open 1st)
7	step back into plié on R with L coupé front
8	step back into plié on L with R coupé front

now facing C1

1-2	2 ballonné devant (L arm high)
3-6	ballotté b,f,b,f
7	assemblé to close 5th
8	changement

26. Piqué arabesques with petit temps de flèshe

Begin SL in tendu efface devant

1	step on R
+	petite temp de flèche devant (left leg pointes devant, switch to R leg devant) (this is a low hitch kick that should just look like pointed feet preparing to piqué)
2	piqué on R in 1st arabesque to SR
3	left will failli through
+	petite temp de flèche (R leg switching to L leg devant)
4	piqué on L in an opposite 1st arabesque to SR
5	R will failli through
+	petite temp de flèche (L leg switching to R leg devant)
6	piqué on R in 1st arabesque to SR
7	roll down into plié arabesque
8	close L leg devant or close L devant in a soutenu turn to the R
1-8	other side going SL

Petite Allegro 6/8 and a Character Turn

27. Pas de chat and détourné

These pas de chats commence with the front foot and close front
1-2	pas de chat R , arms 2nd
3-4	détourné a full turn to the right, arms through 1st to 5th
5-8	repeat

* this can also be done with the opposite arms: 5th to 2nd on pas de chat, to 1st on détourné

Easy 2nd 8 counts
1-2	glissade L
3-4	jeté L,
5-8	pas de bourrée en tournant

Or a quicker 2nd 8
1-2	glissade L
3	jeté L,
4-6	ballotté f,b,f (efface to C2)
7-8	assemblé to L devant 5th

28. Emboité, jetés, and entrechat quatre (begin R foot derrière)
1-4	4 emboité en avant (jump up and land on R, L, R, L with the other foot coupé back)
5-8	glissade and jeté over to the R, glissade and jeté to the L
1-4	repeat 4 emboité en avant
5-8	glissade and assemblé over to the R, 2 entrechat quatre

29. Assemblé de suite - prepare with R derrière

En face
1-2	2 assemblé dessus (over)
3	assemblé derrière (brush to the side, from derrière to derrière, no change)
4	assemblé dessus

Croisé
5	assemblé en avant (to the fourth devant)
6	soubresaut
7	assemblé en arrière (to the fourth derrière)
8	soubresaut
1-8	other side

* repeat all with battu

30. Cabriole and petite jeté

Prepare B+ with R behind
1	step R and cabriole derrière
2	L failli over
3	glissade R
4	jeté over
5-8	other side

Continue R and L or combine with another 8 count combination

31. Character turn

Prepare croisé lunge to C1, R arm on hip, L arm en avant
1-2	inside turn (You could do the style where leg goes to seconde and then retiré.)
	L arm opens and goes to hip. (turning left)
3	after single, put right foot in front sous-sus and détourné to left.
4	finish with L front, step forward into original preparation and continue on same side.

Turns and Across the Floor

1. Beginning chainés
Students should relevé in 1st to prepare. Beginners may place hands on shoulders or hips.
- 1-8   rock in place stepping on r,l,r,l,r,l,r,l
- 9-end   chainé turns across on diagonal
- * variation – 4 rocks, 2 slow chainés, fast chainés the rest of the floor

2. Piqué soutenu turn technique
* To practice right turns from C3 down the diagonal to C1 the student should prepare facing C2 with a small développé to tendu front, the turn will begin with a rond de jambe from front to side.
- 1   ronde from front to side, step out on R pointe or demi pointe
- 2   place L crossing tight in front of R
- 3-4   turn to the R leaving pointes in place, plié 5th

3. Piqué turns
- a.   first time across floor do piqué passés without turning
- b.   2 piqués w/o turning, 2 piqué turns, continue
- c.   2 piqué turns, 1 double piqué turn, continue

4. Pirouette combination
- 1   piqué turn
- 2   piqué soutenu turn
- 3   piqué turn
- 4   lame duck turn (piqué turn en dehors)

5. En dehors close back   3/4 Waltz works well
- 1-4   tombé R en avant, pas de bourrée to 4th en dehors turn R, close 5th back
- 5-8   tombé L en avant, pas be bourrée to 4th en dehors turn L, close 5th back
- Continue: could do singles R and L, doubles R and L; or singles, doubles, triples.

6. En dehors with different endings   3/4 Waltz works well
All these tombés are R en avant
- 1-4   tombé pas de bourrée to 4th, en dehors turn to 4th lunge arms ending high 5th
- 5-8   tombé pas be bourrée to 4th, en dehors turn to 4th lunge arms ending in 2nd
- 1-4   tombé pas de bourrée to 4th, en dehors turn to 4th lunge arabesque arms
- 5-6   tombé pas be bourrée to coupé back
- 7-8   step piqué 1st arabesque hold, failli to croisé derrière

7. En dehors, piqué turns, chainé
- 1+ a2   tombé R en avant, pas de bourrée to 4th
- 3-4   en dehors turn close 5th front
- 5+a6   tombé R en avant, pas de bourrée to 4th
- 7-8   en dehors turn close 5th front
- 1+a2   tombé R en avant, pas de bourrée to 4th
- 3-4   en dehors to 4th (body facing C1)
- 5-6   swivel (turn to the right ending tendu croisé devant to C2)
- 7-8   2 piqué turns (to C1)
- 1-end   chainé turns the rest of the length of the room

8. Chasse, fouetté and piqué turn
- 1-2   chassé en avant with L, arms in front with wrists crossed to C1
- 3-4   kick R front sauté fouetté to 1st arabesque facing C3
- 5-6   turn to the right and chassé with R front (arms extended front with wrists crossed) to C1
- 7-8   Piqué turn on R arms high fifth

9. Piqué, soutenu and en dehors
- 1-2   2 piqué turns
- 3-4   1 piqué soutenu, spot front
- 5-6   en dehors turn from 5th close back
- 7-8   détourné

Waltzes

Across the floor Waltzes – (each count is 3)

These waltzes are generally described for going down the diagonal. Right side is described.
Most can easily be changed to a center combination doing right side then left side.
Many can be used in a circle also. It is very easy to combine these combinations into a dance.
These will often work to the Grand Allegro band on a ballet CD.

1.
1-2	balancé f, b
3-4	waltz turn, (2 waltzes = 1 turn)
5-8	2 piqué turns, 1 double piqué turn

2.
1-4	balancé front, back, front, back
5-8	4 piqué turns (slow)

3.
1-4	2 piqué turns
5-6	sauté on R in 1st arabesque
7-8	half turn to the R sauté on L in 1st arabesque

continue turning to the R into preparation to begin again

4.
1-2	balancé R, L
3-4	waltz turn (2 waltzes=1 turn)
5+a6	tombé front, pas de bourrée to 4th
7-8	en dehors turn, finish back in croisé derrière lunge (arms in arabesque)

5.
1-4	balancé R, L, waltz turning (2 waltzes, 1 turn)
5-6	piqué turn, double piqué turn
7-8	2 (or 4) chainé turns

6.
1-4	balancé R, L, waltz turning (2 waltzes, 1 turn)
5-6	2 lame duck turns (piqué tours en dehors)
7-8	1 double lame duck turn and you are ready for the other side

7.
1-2	balancé R, L
3-4	2 piqué turns
5-6	balancé R, L
7-8	2 pas de chat

8.
1-2	balancé f, b
3-6	2 turning waltzes (4 waltzes = 2 turns)
7	piqué arabesque
+8	plié and relevé in the arabesque
1-2	chassé back to tour jeté
3-4	3 steps back, fouetté
5-6	temps lié back into tendu front croisé
7-8	step on tendu, bring back leg through coupé to tendu front croisé to c2
1-8	piqué turns across floor

9.
1-2-3, 2-2-3	2 balancé turning
3-2-3, 4-2	hop or chug in arabesque on R in plié arms 3rd
	* the arabesque needs to grow as you hop, arms from 1st to 3rd arabesque
-3	failli, (bring the left through to 4th front plié preparation)
5-2-3, 6-2-3	en dehors pirouette, finish back
7-2-3, 8-2-3	en dedans pirouette, finish front

10.
1-2-3, 2-2-3	balancé front, back
3-2-3	piqué arabesque on R
4-2-3	close L in 5th front plié, détourné to the right to relevé R 5th front
5-2-3, 6-2-3	tombé pas de bourrée
7-2-3, 8-2-3	glissade , grand jeté

Waltzes

11. 1-2-3, 2-2-3   balancé écarté R f and L back
     3-2-3, 4-2-3   turning waltz
     5-2-3   piqué arabesque on R (tombé L over on 3),
     6-2-3   pas de bourrée (back R, step left to left, R front)
     7-2-3   step L to Left, step R behind in reverse soutenu (turning R)
     8-2-3   balancé L
     repeats on same side

12. 1, 2   2 piqué turns to the R
     3   lunge R to R,(L is tendu to the L) arms go 3rd arabesque (w/ head R)
     4   then L arm swings low until arms are in 1st arabesque (head looking L)
     5,6   2 piqué turns to the left
     7,8   lunge L port de bras to the L

13. * combination 11   8 counts - R side
       combination 12   8 counts - R and L
       repeat
* teach to the front, then this makes a nice step for a large circle

14. 1   sauté (or piqué if slower) in attitude croisé devant
     2   tombé into turning pas de bourrée
     3-4   repeat
     5-6   tombé pas de bourrée into 4th preparation
     7-8   en dehors pirouette

15. 1-2   pas de basque R
     3-4   pas de basque L
     5-6   pas de basque R into sauté in 2nd arabesque on L
     7-8   bring R leg devant into soutenu turn to the L
     1-8   other side
     1-2   développé R devant with relevé
     3-4   tombé on R, and relevé in 1st arabesque
     5-6   tour jeté back
     7-8   right out of the tour jeté step back on L and développé R devant with relevé
     1-8   tombé on R, pas de bourrée, glissade, grand jeté

16. 1-2-3, 2-2-3   turning waltz
     3-2-3   piqué 1st arabesque, failli on 3
     4-2-3   relevé développé R efface devant – tombé on R-pull L in front up to sous-sus
     5-2-3, 6-2-3   balancé L and R
     7-2   temp lie back to tendu R croisé devant to C2
       -3   tombé forward into preparation
     8-2-3   en dedans pirouette
     Continues same direction

17. Center Combination
     1-2-3, 2-2-3   balancé R, balancé L
     3-2-3   sauté 1st arabesque on R to C1, close front
     4-2-3   détourné to C2
     5-2-3   balancé L to C3
     6-2-3   ballonné R to C1 (R leg goes out to seconde, into retiré and back out to 2nd)
                     R arm is high (écarté)
     7   tombé into 1st arabesque arm is high 5th
       -2-3, 8-2-3   hop backwards toward C3 in arabesque (little chugs in plié)
                     R arm comes down the front and circles into arabesque
     1-8   other side

Grand Allegro

Note: *All of this Grand Allegro work is done going across the floor in a diagonal.*
The first side begins on the R and goes from C3 to C1,
The second side is done from C4 to C2.
If the combination tells which foot, it is describing the 1st side.

Beginning grand allegro – simple repetition
** I realize these do not really qualify as combinations, but repeated sautés build more
strength than sautés with a combination of steps.*

1. Just chassé across floor. (will not change) R foot front from corner 3.

2. Just sauté in 1st arabesque. (will alternate)

3. Chassé arms in 1st, sauté in 1st arabesque. (will alternate)

4. Chassé arms in 1st, cabriole in 1st arabesque

5. Glissade, pas de chat, glissade, saut de chat

6. Pas de chat, grand jeté with développé, pas de chat, grand jeté développé

7. Sauté in 1st arabesque, step L leg over, glissade R, assemblé over

** The above steps work great with all of the students in a circle. That way no one is waiting and the
students can do many consecutively.   This is an efficient use of time and students think it is fun.

8.   Tour jeté exercise for technique – no jumping - 4 slow counts for accuracy
prepare R tendu back facing C3– arms in second

1	turn toward C1 chassé de cote with the R
2	step R, battement front with the L, arms low 5th - through 1st to high 5th
3	fouetté to the right to face C3 with the L leg in arabesque, arms stay in 5th
4	jump to switch the legs and the arms may open to 2nd or arabesque

Use this exercise to gain strength holding the height of the leg during the fouetté.
It also teaches not to bring the arms down too soon so the jump will have height.

9.   Arabesques with grand jeté

1-2	chassé-sauté arabesque R
3-4	chassé-sauté arabesque L
5-6	step R, step L, grand jeté R
7-8	step L, piqué on R in 1st arabesque holding, circle arms to 2nd arabesque and run off

10.   Variation on 9, zig-zags from side to side

1-2	chassé-sauté arabesque R
3-4	chassé-sauté arabesque L
5-6	step R, step L, grand jeté R
7-8	contretemps and begin other side

11.   Arabesques with assemblé en tournant

1-2	chassé-sauté arabesque R
3-4	chassé-sauté arabesque L
5-6	chassé piqué arabesque on R
7-8	chassé back on L - assemblé en tournant
	(step to back corner on L, assemblé with R turning to the L, landing R front in 5th)

12.   Sissonne en avant

1-4	2 sissonne front fermé
5	sissonne front ouverte
6	step L though to the front, R leg coupé back
7+8	pas de bourrée en tournant

13. Grand jeté - repeat around in a circle to the right

1	sauté arabesque on R
2	failli
3	glissade R
4	grand jeté R

14. Sautés with passé

1	sauté first arabesque on R
2	sauté on L -R leg in passé w/ R arm high, head to the L
3,4	repeat 1-2
5-8	tombé pas de bourrée, glissade, grand jeté
1-4	piqué first arabesque, chassé back, step L battement R front sauté, fouetté into back attitude
5-8	pull attitude down to coupé, tombé pas de bourrée, glissade, grand jeté.

15. Grand allegro - basic elements

1-4	piqué arabesque, failli, glissade, grand jeté (to C1)
5-8	repeat 1-4
1-4	piqué arabesque, tour jeté land plié (to C3)
5-8	relevé in arabesque, tour jeté (to C3)
1-2	step on L, tendu R devant to C2 (prepare)
3-8+	piqué turns the length of the floor (to C1)

16. Pas de chats

1+a2	tombé, pas de bourrée,
+3	glissade
4	pas de chat
5-7	tombé, pas de bourrée, glissade
8	grand pas de chat

17. Variations on 16

* change the tombé on 1 of the next 8 to contretemps to change sides and it can zig-zag across floor
* vary the jumps on 4 and 8: pas de chat - grand jeté or pas de chat - saut de chat or grand jeté - grand jeté, etc.
* change the tombé, pas de bourrée to:
  +1-soubresaut, chassé, + a 2-pas de bourrée:
  (soubresaut in 5th, as you land chassé forward into a low arabesque, then pas de bourrée.)
* add a développé on the preparation count 8
  (step back into fondu coupé front and développé effacé devant with relevé)

18. Grand jetés and tour jetés

1-2	développé front leg croisé (L) relevé, chassé L en avant
3-4	step L R, grand jeté croisé, land in plié back attitude
5-6	piqué first arabesque on R, chassé L en avant
7-8	step L R, grand jeté croisé, land in plié back attitude
1-2	piqué first arabesque on R
3-4	tour jeté back
5-8	another piqué arabesque, tour jeté

19. Sautés in battement and tour jetés

1	step sauté on the R with left a la quatrième devant 90, arms high 3rd
2	balancé turning R (step L, R, L)
3,4	repeat
5-8	tombé pas de bourrée glissade pas de chat
1-2	step R, L piqué arabesque on R
3-4	tour jeté
5-6	tour jeté
7-8	step on L, tendu R devant to C2 (prepare)
1-8+	chainé turns the length of the floor

Grand Allegro

20. Intermediate grand allegro

1-2	glissade front over, cabriole devant (L arm high) fermé
3-4	glissade back, cabriole back
+5	failli, sauté 1st arabesque
+6	failli, tombé pas de bourrée
7-8	glissade, grand jeté

21. Advanced with grand pas de chat – prepare L tendu front croisé to C1

7-8 of intro	step on L, battement R à la seconde écarté
	arm through écarté to high 5th
	R leg comes down to coupé front plié, arm to mid 5th
1-2	chassé (arms 3rd), sauté de basque (arms mid 5th)
3-4	repeat
5-6	cabriole back
7-8	chassé back fouetté
1-2	chassé back fouetté
3-4	3 steps to sous-sus
5-8	tombé pas de bourrée glissade, grand pas de chat

grand pas de chat = 1st knee up, 1st leg straightens as 2nd knee goes up close 5th

22. Lame ducks, soutenu turn, tour jeté, and more

Facing C1

1-2	lame duck (piqué turn en dehors, step down on R, piqué on L to the R)
3-4	lame duck (end your turn with R in retiré front)
5-6	développé R devant, step down on it into 1st arabesque plié
	(the développé is small, the stretch in arabesque is big)
7-8	bring L leg to the front and soutenu turn to the R
1-8	repeat
1	ballotté a terre to tendu efface devant - L arm front in 3rd
2	ballotté a terre to tendu efface derrière - arms like 1st arabesque
	(this is not a big jump, but a placing of the legs front and back going through coupé)
3-5	tour jeté back
6-7	repeat the ballotté front and back
8-2	tour jeté
3-4	chassé L en avant to tendu croisé derrière
5-8	pivot to the R to tendu croisé devant to C2, (L arm is high in 4th)
1-16	chainé turns to C1

* the counts may change with different tempos of music, you may like this with medium allegro music.

23. Prepare in 5th R foot devant, may need to start on 8

+1	temps levé, chassé into 1st arabesque in fondu
+a2	pas de bourrée
+3+4	2- 90° ballonné R leg devant, L arm high in 3rd
5+a6	tombé on R, pas de bourrée into croisé lunge
7-8	en dehors pirouette finish with R back in lunge
1-8	repeat – this time temps levé out of the lunge with R passing through coupé into chassé
1	piqué on R in 1st arabesque
2-3	chassé tour jeté toward the back diagonal
4	step back (tombé) on L, fondu with R in coupé, développé R devant with relevé
5	tombé forward into 1st arabesque, then relevé
6-7	chassé, tour jeté
8	step back (tombé) on L, fondu with R in coupé, développé R devant with relevé
1	tombé forward out of the développé
+a2	pas de bourrée
3-8	glissade, grand jeté 3x (may use saut de chat, a grand jeté with développé of front leg)

24. Grand allegro

1-2	Balancé R and L
3-4	2 steps (RL) and grand jeté R
5-6	2 steps (LR) and grand jeté L
7-8	2 steps (RL) and piqué 1st arabesque on R
1-6	3 massive steps back toward C3 and tour jeté
7-8	3 steps toward C3 (LRL), pointe R front to C2 (turn preparation)
1-6	6 piqué turns (single, single, double, single, single, double)
7-8	chasse forward into tendu derrière (like 1st arabesque) and hold

25. Cabrioles

Prepare in B+ on the R leg

1-2	cabriole devant
	(step forward on the L and brush the R devant with the L leg beating underneath)
3-4	cabriole derrière
	(step forward on the R into sauté 1st arabesque with the R beating underneath)
5+6	step L, R, L
7-8	piqué on R in first arabesque
1 ---	failli L forward out of the arabesque to begin again

26. Character allegro – can be done in a circle

1-2-3	temps de flesh devant R, step L, step R
2-2-3	temps de flesh devant L, step R , step L
3-2-3	cabriole R devant, 3 steps
4-2-3	cabriole L devant, 2 steps
5-2-3	step L and hop in plié while R développés devant, L arm slowly first and open
6-2-3	same on R
7-2-3, 8-2-3	2 steps grand jeté R arms 1st port de bras with palms up
same L	

27. Ballotté combination from Giselle Act 1

On the ballotté the arms are in 3rd devant in opposition.
Ballotté is light and springy, always go in and out of cou de pied.

1	ballotté effacé devant to C1(right front)
2	ballotté effacé derrière (left back)
3-4	repeat
5	failli (left comes forward and step on it)
6	ballonné effacé devant (right front) arms to first
7	step forward on R
8	grand jeté croisé (jeté with L) arms to an extended open first
1-8	now other side to C2

28. Grand allegro with cabriole - from downstage corner C1 to C3

Prepare in B+ on L

1-2-3	step back on R and brush L back for cabriole derrière
2-2-3	large balancé moving back L R L
3-2-3	piqué on R to the R toward C3 - do a 1 ½ piqué attitude derrière turn
4-2	end facing C1 stretch into plié arabesque,
-3	failli L forward to start again

29. Sissonnes – from the back of the room moving downstage

1-2	sissonne en avant fermé - 1st arabesque
3-4	sissonne en arrière fermé - effacé (downstage arm high)
5-7	3 sissonnes en avant (2 fermé, and 3rd ouverte)
8	close front in fifth and change corners

Grand Allegro

30. Sissonne, failli, assemblé over - down the diagonal

The épaulment changes on the sissonne and on the assemblé in this combination. After the student understands the steps and the changing épaulment, encourage them to make it very large.

Prepare in 5th with the R foot front to C2

1   sissonne en avant ouverte - into 1st arabesque facing C1

2   failli - the left leg comes through to fourth – still to C1

3-4   assemblé through 2nd and close front to C2

       (the R leg brushes front as the body pivots and you are in seconde in the air and then close front to C2)

continue with the same side

32. Sissonne changée, failli, assemblé en avant
     from the back of the room moving downstage on the diagonals

The épaulment changes on the sissonne in this combination.

Prepare in 5th with the R foot front to C2

1   sissonne changée en avant ouverte - into a croisé arabesque on L facing C1

2   failli - the right leg comes through to fourth – to C1

3-4   assemblé through 4nd en avant and close front - still to C1

       (the L leg brushes en avant and closes front)

continue changing sides

Here are some choreography ideas for pairs. This one can be for a boy and girl, or for sets of girls.

1. Cabrioles - face each other, with sides to the audience
Dancer 1

1-2	cabriole devant with the R
3	step forward on R with L extended back
4	step back on L with R extended front
5-6	step down on R and cabriole devant with L
7	step forward on L with R extended back
8	step back on R with L extended front

Dancer 2

1-2	cabriole derrière with the L
3	step back on L with R extended front
4	step forward on R with L extended back
5-6	step down on L and cabriole derrière with R
7	step back on R with L extended front
8	step forward on L with R extended back

This is cute with just one couple or several sets going around in a circle.
The arms are in opposition 3rds, because they were very close together, have one arm out in seconde and the other arm in front with the elbow bent.   The bodies tilt back and forth together.

2. Sissonnes - face each other both with R front
Dancer 1

1	sissonne en avant fermé
2	sissonne en arrière fermé
3	sissonne en avant ouverte
4	pas de bourrée (en tournant optional)

Dancer 2

1	sissonne en arrière fermé
2	sissonne en avant fermé
3	sissonne en arrière ouverte
4	pas de bourrée (en tournant optional)

or
Dancer 1 could go sissonne front, back, front, back, R, L, R, L
Dancer 2_ sissonnes back, front, back, front, L, R, L, R

3. Group sissonnes that change lines - face the audience

```
        B     B     B     B

           A     A     A
```

Group B

1	sissonne en avant
2	sous-sus
3	sissonne en arrière
4	sous-sus

Group A

1	sissonne en arrière
2	sous-sus
3	sissonne en avant
4	sous-sus

or if your students cannot sissonne large enough to pass each other change to

Group B

1-2	2 sissonne en avant
3+4	pas de bourrée or changement, entrechat quatre or sissonnes right and left

Group A - do the sissonnes opposite
Now both reverse to switch lines back.

Reverence

1. 2 simple curtsies
Prepare in B+ on the L leg – arms fifth en bas (bras bas)

1	step to the R with the R (L will be in tendu à la seconde) arms go through en avant and open seconde
2	take the L leg to the back to be in the other B+
3	curtsy, arms lower to demi seconde
4	stretch the supporting knee and arms move to bras bas

Now other side

2. Reverence with fondu instead of curtsy
5th En face

1-4	first port de bras
	1 arms from low to first position
	2 arms open seconde
	3-4 slowly lower arms to en bas, head and eyes slightly lowering
5-8	repeat
1-4	port de bras en dehors through high 5th (first, fifth, seconde, en bas)
5-8	port de bras en dedans through high 5th (seconde, fifth, first, en bas)
1	tendu R à la seconde
2	pivot and step on R to stage R into first arabesque
3	L leg comes through first and arms to first
4	through to tendu devant (croisé) with arms high fifth
5-6	fondu in the tendu and port de bras back, arms can stay high fifth or open seconde
7-8	recover to a straight back and close fifth
1-8	last 8 to the other side

3. My favorite reverence
Prepare in B+ on the L leg – arms fifth en bas (bras bas)

1-2	step with the R to the R, L goes to B+ - arms through first to seconde
3	put L in fourth croisé derrière and plié - arms to first
4	temps lié to croisé tendu devant to C2 - arms high 3rd
5-8	port de bras forward (cambré) with fondu - L arm does a wash
	This "wash" is the rare time in ballet where the elbow bends as the L hand moves rather close to the body from head to toe. Keep arm long as you come up from the cambré.
1	shift weight forward into croisé lunge. (I slide the tendu front leg slightly forward before planting it in a deep plié – just to make a broader lunge) arms open seconde
2	cambré forward in the lunge arms reach low 5th
3-4	raise back - still in lunge – arms to first
5-6	cambré back in lunge – downstage arm goes to high 5th and back - so arms are in fourth
7-8	recover to tendu croisé derrière - arms in seconde
1-16	now step to the left and repeat this sequence on the other side

1-2   step to the R in B+ - R arm reaches straight up – palm out
3-8   fold down into a very deep curtsy where the back knee tucks behind the front knee. The R arm bends and pulls down straight in front of the face and circles to the side as you rise up.
1-8   do this same "princess" curtsy on the L

The butterfly
The easiest and most popular is to sit on the floor, put the soles of the feet together, pressing knees toward the floor.   Do not let the student pull up on their toes which would sickle their feet.

Butterfly extension
To further work on turn-out have the student try to lift their heels while in the butterfly. Begin straightening the legs and try to hold the heels up as long as possible until the legs are fully extended front.

The frog
The butterfly on its' stomach. The student lays on their stomach with knees pulled up to the sides. While laying and stretching try to press feet toward ground, alternately and simultaneously.

Any time you take a barre exercise and do it on the floor, there is great benefit to correct positioning and alignment. In any exercise lying on your back, make sure the small of the back is pressed to the ground, and not arched. Make sure both shoulders and hips stay on the ground. This allows no slouching with développé devant, helps the student learn not to arch, and helps show them their correct placement in second.

The L
The butterfly and the frog are stretches, the L builds strength. Lay on the ground with straight legs pointing toward the ceiling. Legs are pointed and parallel. This is an excellent way to gain strength and ensure the student is turning out from the hip and not the feet. This is important for any student who tends to turn-out more with their feet than they should, and have the resulting patella problems.

1-4	turn-out from the hip (legs are in first)
5-8	relax back to parallel
1-4	turn-out
5-8	turn-in to parallel
1-16	repeat 2 more times
1-32	repeat with flexed feet

Passé développé – laying on back

Right leg	1-2	passé
	3-4	développé devant
	5-6	hold and turn-out (student can pull on leg to stretch more)
	7-8	lower
Left leg	1-8	same
Repeat		

Now repeat à la seconde

Grand battement - laying on back

Right	1-8	4 battement devant
Left	1-8	4 battement devant
Right	1-8	4 battement à la seconde
Left	1-8	4 battement à la seconde

Grand battement - laying on stomach

Right	1-8	4 battement derrière
Left	1-8	4 battement derrière
	1-6	push up with your arms to stretch your back
	7-8	lower
	1-8	same back stretch w/o the arms (you can put them behind back or in 5th)

Batterie exercise – on back with legs pointed toward ceiling and turned out

1-6	legs cross in 5th like they would in a beat: beat R front, L front, R, L, R, L
7-8	open to seconde

repeat many times

More Turn-Out Exercises

1. The Cou-de-pied turn-out workout - center

Begin in 5th with the R foot front

1	peel R foot up to sur le cou-de-pied devant
2	move it to the wrapped position
3	move it to sur le cou-de-pied derrière
4	place the foot in back in fifth (toe-ball-heel)
5-8	repeat with the left foot
1-24	continue en arrière R L R L R L
1-36	repeat all moving en avant

2. Passé turnout - face the barre in first - medium to slow speed

1-2	R leg to passé
3-4	turn in passé across body
5-6	turn passé back to side
7-8	développé side
1-2	retiré to passé
3-4	turn in across body
5-6	turn out
7-8	close first

1-2	tendu R and put down in large seconde position
3-4	plié deeply - stay down
5-6	body moves to R as left leg becomes straight
7-8	staying low flex the left foot for more stretch
1-4	move body thru plié center to the L and then flex the R
5-8	rise out of plié into tendu R and close back

1-32	repeat the whole combination starting L

3. This tendu really works the turnout

1	tendu front (don't close)
2	put the heel down in fourth
3-4	pull the leg into fifth position keeping the heel on the floor (use your turn-out muscles)
1-12	continue en croix
1	tendu front
2	turn in
3	turn out
4	close
1-12	continue en croix

Music Suggestions

This is a list of some of my favorite CD's for the ballet class. I did not suggest a piece of music for each combination because the options are endless. You may use your personal preference for the tempo you would like. I like to change music regularly and increase tempos as the students are able. These CD's are available through www.danceclassmusic.com .

Behind Barres by Judy Rice and Paul Lewis - Volumes 1, 2, or 3
I recommend any Behind Barres CD. The tracks match the categories in The Ballet Combination Book really well. They have long tracks so you can do both sides without changing the music. Sometimes the tendu or dégagé band will repeat with an increased tempo which is a fun challenge for students.

Music For Ballet Class by Suki Schorer & Nancy McDill
This is an excellent CD for a basic technique class. It has a track for en dehors and a track for en dedans pirouettes. Whenever I need to start kids on the basics of pirouettes I get out this one.

Music For Ballet Class by Olga Evreinoff & Lynn Stanford
This is another favorite I use regularly for beginning - intermediate.

Inspired by Music by David Stein & Kristine Elliott This is another quality CD I have enjoyed.

Tune In and Turn Out by Judy Rice and Paul Lewis (Behind Barres)
This CD uses novelty tunes from old TV shows in the categories of pliés, tendus, etc. This is a fun change for students of any age.

Music and Mistle Toes by Steven Mitchell
I use this in December. It makes class extra special to have Christmas music. By the quality of this CD, I would expect to enjoy any Steven Mitchell CD. It has all the categories I like and long tracks.

Simplified Ballet Terms

* when there is an accent mark slanted up over the e it sounds like a long a.

Basic Barre Terms:

Grand Plié –   full bending of the knees

Demi Plié –   small bending of the knees, heels must stay on the ground

Battement -   beating, basically a moving of the leg forward, side, or back

Battement Tendu –   battement stretched, the leg moves out to a stretched pointed position without leaving the floor.

Battement Dégagé –   battement disengaged, battement that leaves the floor 1 to 2 inches

Ronde de jambe –   round with the leg.

        A terre – on the ground

        En l'air – in the air

        En dehors – to the outside

        En dedans – to the inside

Battement Frappé –   battement struck, a movement usually from sur le cou de pied, striking the floor as the leg extends.

Développé – The unfolding of the leg, usually from 5th to passé and then extended

Sur le cou de pied – on the neck of the foot

Fondu – to melt, a plié on one leg, like to tendu or coupé with a plié

Grand battement - Large battement

Relevé - to rise (to the half-toe in slippers or full pointe en pointe)

En croix – in the shape of a cross, to do an exercise front, side, back, side

En cloche – a movement of the leg from devant to derrière (or reverse) through 1st

Center

Adagio – slow sustained movements

Petite Allegro – small quick movements, a combination made up of sautés

        Sauté - jumped, or jumping

        Temps levé – jump from one foot to the same foot

        Jeté – thrown, a jump from 1 foot to the other foot

        Sissonne – a jump from 2 feet to 1

        Assemblé – to assemble, a jump from 1 foot to 2 feet

        Pas de Chat – jump of the Cat

        Changement – jump in fifth changing feet

        Entrechat - braided

Positions and Directions

Devant– a position to the front

En Avant – moving to the front

Derrière – a position to the back

En Arrière – moving to the back

À la seconde – to the side

De côté – moving side to side

Croisé - a diagonal position to a corner where the legs are crossed

Effacé – a diagonal position to a corner where the legs are not crossed

Écarté – position to the side on a diagonal

En face – facing the audience

Pirouette and Turn Directions

En Dehors – to the outside, turning away from the standing leg (a turn on your R will go L)

En Dedans – to the inside, turning toward the standing leg (a turn on your R will go R)

Counting in French - un, deux, trios, quatre, cinq, six

Pas de deux – step for two

Pas de trios – step for three

Entrechat trois – braided three times

Entrechat quatre – braided four times

Reproducible handout

Dance Teacher press

Ballet Step by Step, The Pointe Class Book, Recital Notes,
Educational Posters, Ballet Teminology Banners and Wallpaper Border,
Ballet and Tap Coloring Sheets, Ballet and Tap Flashcards,
Dance Charm Jewelry and so much more.